Pinoys at War

Relative Deprivation, Motivation, and the Filipino Guerillas of World War II

By

Matthew C. Andres

ISBN 978-0-578-11844-4

For Tracy.

Forever.

Prologue: December, 1941

It was the week before Christmas, 1941, when First Sergeant Jose first killed another human being. Jose was the senior non-commissioned officer of M Company, 1st Infantry Regiment of the Philippine Commonwealth Army. Jose was a rarity in the Philippine Army: an educated, thoughtful man in an army that had been thrown together helter-skelter. Educated as an industrial arts teacher, Jose had briefly taught at a Manila-area high school before joining the army in 1939, drawn by the steady pay and career path of a professional soldier.

The pre-war Philippine Commonwealth Army was composed of a small cadre of professional soldiers, while the bulk of the army was made up of conscripts. Juachon was quickly signaled out for advanced rank, and was sent to a non-commissioned officer academy. He graduated six months later with the rank of First Sergeant; the senior enlisted soldier in his company. While in the NCO academy, Jose excelled. He had been asked to stay on for a further three months training, with the promise of an officer's commission.

Jose readily accepted the chance to move up the ranks, and secure a future for his family. As events so often out-pace dreams, his commission was not to be. The Imperial Japanese Empire invaded the Philippines on 8 December 1941. The Academy closed down, with all personnel returning to their respective units. First Sergeant Jose rushed back to M Company, steadying his poorly trained troops as they deployed for war.

In the weeks that followed 8 December, the combined Filipino-American forces had done nothing but retreat. Down the length of Luzon, the Philippines' main island, the Philippine Army repeatedly stood and faced the Japanese invaders. Each time the poorly trained, ill equipped Filipinos would be forced back by the combined arms of the Imperial Japanese Army. In these cases, Jose's M Company—a heavy machine gun company—would lay down suppressive fire, trying to pin the Japanese with a shower of bullets as the rest of the army retreated.

It was after one of these retreats, called "retrograde movements" by the army, that Jose killed his first Japanese invader. Night had fallen, and Jose had finished checking on his men: ensuring they stayed awake on guard duty; making sure their fox-holes were dug deep enough. Lacking barbed wire or sandbags, Jose had ordered his soldiers to string vines horizontally across M Company's frontage, at roughly knee height. The men had been subsisting on rice and canned salmon. The empty salmon cans were hung from the vines, with pebbles dropped inside. The idea was that the Japanese troops would trip over the vines, and the pebbles rattling in the tin cans would alert the Filipino troops.

The idea, unfortunately, failed that night. After returning to his fox-hole in the middle of M Company's perimeter, Jose had just fallen asleep when the soldier sharing the foxhole shook Jose awake. The soldier, a professional boxer from Manila, said he heard footsteps coming from *behind* M Company's position.

Jose strained to hear, and could faintly make out the sound of footsteps on fallen leaves. In the moonlight, Jose and the boxer could see Japanese soldiers stealthily moving down the path. Their leader carried a samurai sword, with a shiny blade that reflected the moonlight.

Later, while on the run as a guerrilla leader, Jose would learn not to fire during night ambushes, because the flash of the gunfire would reveal his position—instead, they would throw explosives. But on that night, First Sergeant Jose did the only thing he could: he pulled his pistol from his holster and shot the Japanese leader. The boxer followed Jose's lead, swinging his machine gun around and mowing down the rest of the Japanese patrol.

Sixty-eight years later, in the comfort of his Chicago apartment, Jose related to me that he relived that moment every night of his life.

Chapter One: Introduction

In the social sciences, it is often hard to assign "beginning" and "end" dates to political events. The flow of time often conspires to confound the researcher's attempts at classification. Such is the case of the Philippines, a country that seems to always be resisting *someone* or *something.* From their earliest days, when they resisted the Chinese; to the fateful day in 1521, when a small tribe killed Ferdinand Magellan and ensured the return of the Spanish; to the present day Moro Islamic Liberation Front—the Filipinos always seem to be resisting outside forces. Indeed, their national heroes are those who led a guerrilla-type lifestyle: dozens of Philippine towns are named for the nationalist leader Jose Rizal; and Filipinos still speak reverentially of Nino Aquino's murder on the tarmac of Manila Airport. Both men, it is worth noting, were killed by the forces they resisted.

In this book, I have attempted to document one such period of Filipino resistance; specifically, the armed defense of the Philippines against the Japanese Empire during World War Two. My initial thesis involved the motivations and expectations of guerrillas in the Philippines, analyzing the movement through the lens of tested political violence models. The deeper I delved into the subject, the more I realized I was facing the researcher's dilemma mentioned above—where to begin and where to end. One cannot write of the anti-Japanese guerrillas without understanding the defeated Filipino-American army from whence the guerrillas came. One cannot write of the heartbreaking failure of that Filipino-American army without understanding its role within a Commonwealth political system. Most importantly, I realized that to truly accomplish the mission of my thesis statement, I would need to attempt to understand the individual Filipinos who joined the resistance. In short, I found that the solution was not one of understanding a specific place in time; rather it was a question of tailoring the methodology to understand the people of that time.

Books abound analyzing insurgent warfare, but this book was never intended to turn on the hinges of books; it was meant to be driven by *soul*. It seems quite obvious that, in order to understand the motivations and expectations of Filipino guerilla warriors, one must seek out and speak to the Filipino guerrillas themselves. In the Filipino community, this short time span—1941 to 1945—is a sort of ethnic salad days. They were days of bravery and sacrifice; of absurdity and melancholy; and of terror and eventual victory. To the Filipinos who survived it, the Second World War is the yardstick against which they measure their lives and self worth. Throughout the research for this book, I traveled to many of the Filipino communities in Illinois, and had the honor of speaking with these men and women whose youth was spent—quite literally—defeating the Japanese invaders. In retirement homes, American Legion Posts, restaurants, and Filipino community centers, I had the honor to listen to these veterans explain, in sing-song accented English, why they did as they did.

Though this work is academic in nature, one cannot write effectively if one does not have an emotional stake in the work. I did not seek to answer the Historian's question of "why" the war occurred, but rather to answer a question of motivation; and in this case, the guerillas' faith. I wanted to know why the

Pinoys, as the Filipinos call themselves, continued fighting after all was lost. I wanted to know *how* they kept the fight going, how they kept the faith, through three long years in the jungle.

Finally, as a second generation Filipino-American that has never been to the Philippines and speaks halting *Pilipino* with a Chicago accent, I wanted to know *who* these men and women were. I wanted to see (quite desperately, at times) the soul of these World War Two veterans, who once traveled a path the rest of us can never fully understand. The result of my research is this book.

Chapter Two: Historiography

Historiography of the Bataan Campaign

To begin the project, I focused my survey of the Historiography into three main sections: A) works that focus on the mechanics of insurgent warfare; B) historical works about World War Two Philippines; and C) major political science volumes dealing with political violence.

On the subject of insurgent warfare the best book is Walter Laqueur's *Guerrilla: A Historical and Critical Study.* Laqueur's research covers the history of insurgent warfare from biblical times through the Irish Republican Army campaigns of the 1970's. The most startling aspect of *Guerrilla* is that Laqueur does not really have a central thesis. Rather, he believes that insurgent movements are so diverse as to defy categorizing.

Counter Guerrilla Operations: the Philippine Experience, written by Colonels Napoleon Valeriano and Charles Bohannon, was another insightful study of guerrilla warfare. Valeriano, a World War II Filipino veteran, had fought against the Japanese as a guerrilla. Later, he commanded an elite Filipino infantry unit during counter-guerrilla operations against the *Hukbalahap*. Valeriano's insight into guerrilla warfare is chilling, as some of the post-war Filipino anti-guerrilla tactics, used against their countrymen, were culled from the Imperial Japanese Army.

With the ongoing US military operations in Iraq and Afghanistan, a flurry of books have been written about insurgencies, many of dubious quality. Among the best of the current crop is *Chasing Ghosts: Unconventional Warfare in American History*, by Professor John Tierney. Tierney's expertise is in insurgent warfare in Central America during the first half of the twentieth century, and his chapters on Nicaragua and Sandino are the most in-depth in the book, and have the most bearing on the Philippine guerrilla experience.

Also valuable is *Beating Goliath: Why Insurgencies Win*, by Professor Jeffrey Record. Record addresses the concept of "will" in achieving victory in insurgent wars. Record proffers that the side with the greater organizational will to win will most often prevail. Occupying armies generally lack the greater will, since they have less to achieve in defeating the guerrilla force (as the occupier always has a home to return to).

In addition to mainstream works on insurgencies and guerrilla warfare, the US military has produced countless volumes on their own. Though created for a narrow readership (professional soldiers), these technical- and field-manuals proved to be valuable tools in my research. The bulk of them were written during the Viet Nam War, or post-war by soldiers whose operational combat experience was in Southeast Asia. As such, they tend to be heavy on anti-Communist methodology. Still, many Army manuals were written with input by Social Science professionals, and their methodology will be familiar to any Historian or Political Scientist. Among the most impactful volumes were: Counterinsurgency (FM 3-24); Counterguerrilla Operations (FM 90-8); and Human Factors Considerations of Undergrounds in Insurgencies (Department of the Army Pamphlet 550-104).

In this project, historiography and research methodology are closely related, with the availability of the former influencing the operation of the latter. The historical works written about the Bataan Campaign is incredibly sparse. I say "incredibly" because World War Two is one of the most-studied subjects in American history. Despite multiple television channels with programming devoted to World War Two history, and World War Two movies consistently being top grossing films, Bataan has been largely forgotten.[1] Even more tragic, is that the personal stories of the *Pinoys* has been forgotten, as each day sees hundreds of these veterans passing.

In mining the historiography of the Bataan Campaign, I have found two truly excellent books dealing with the military operations. The first is the official history, written by the US Army immediately after the war. The author, Louis Morton, was an army historian serving in the Philippines during World War

---

[1] One exception is the Hollywood blockbuster "The Great Raid." Like history, the movie marginalized the role of the Filipino guerrillas. One veteran I interviewed became visibly agitated at the mention of the movie, as he despised it so very much.

Two. Written and published at a time when most career military officers were churning out self-serving wartime memoirs, Morton's volume stands out as an example of academic integrity. Morton was not hesitant to point out the failures of the politicians and officers tasked with defending the Philippines.

The second book is *Bataan: Our Last Ditch* by John Whitman. Whitman, a professional army officer, wrote a massive, well documented book that places the Bataan Campaign within the greater matrix of the Pacific War. If there is a (minor) failing in Whitman's excellent book, it is the failure to incorporate the stories of enlisted Filipino soldiers. This failing is not one of Americentricity, rather it is the inevitable outcome of Whitman's training. As a high ranking army officer, his inclination is to follow the stories of the planners and commanders, not the average foot soldier.

In addition to those two histories, a great many sources exist on the Bataan Death March: the roughly 80 mile forced march of the starving American and Filipino prisoners, enforced by their Japanese captors.

Unfortunately, the vast historiography blatantly overlooks the Filipino's suffering during the Death March. Instead, these sources paint the incident as being an American affair—despite the fact that approximately 80 Filipinos died for every American death during the march.

There are a few first-hand memoirs that document Filipino actions during the war. Most of these are written by white American officers who commanded elite Philippine Scout units. These memoirs are valuable because officers assigned to the Philippine Scouts tended to be among the best and brightest. They had spent considerable time in their duty positions, and were well acquainted with Filipino soldiers and their culture. The best of these memoirs is *Anytime, Anywhere*, by John Olson. Olson was a battalion staff officer with the 57th Infantry—the Philippine Scout regiment that saw the most fighting during Bataan.

Another great officer's memoir is *Lieutenant Ramsey's War,* by Edwin Ramsey. Ramsey served in the 26th Cavalry Regiment, composed of American officers and Filipino soldiers. Ramsey would lead a mounted cavalry charge at Moron—the last mounted charge in history by the US Cavalry. Much like Olson, Ramsey saw considerable hard fighting on Bataan, and as a guerrilla leader he fought until liberation.

Few first hand memoirs exist written by Filipinos. In three years of searching, all the while communicating with Filipino veterans' groups, I was only able to find two Filipino memoirs. The first, *Rays of a Setting Sun,* was written by Eliseo Rio, a graduate of the Philippine Military Academy. It tells the fascinating tale of a rookie officer who had to learn his grisly trade while fighting the long retreat to Bataan. On the opposite end of the spectrum is *All This Was Bataan,* by Silvestre Tagarao. Tagarao was a draftee with little training when he was first sent into combat. Both Rio and Tagarao would end up in the guerrillas.

This dearth of *Pinoy* memoirs tells more about the cultural differences than literary differences. During the war, the Philippines suffered to a far greater extent than the United States. After Warsaw, Manila was the allied capital city with the most destruction. On a personal level, nearly every Filipino had friends or family killed, or property destroyed by the Japanese. For the Filipinos, World War Two didn't have such a happy ending. They didn't have America's prosperous 1950's, with suburban houses and a car in the garage. Instead, they had a ruined economy with no industrial base; agriculture that would take decades to produce at pre-war levels; and the ever lingering accusations of collaboration.

Chapter Three: Field Research

With complete candor I must state that my methodology was nothing groundbreaking. I utilized standard techniques drawn from the fields of oral history and political science. Primarily, I sought to use the existing historiography as a framework; a sort of social science skeleton. The initial battle for the Philippines took five months; there really isn't any significant military insight that I could add. I knew from the beginning of the project that the "unit of study" would be Filipino veterans who had fought as guerrillas; thus my primary goal was seeking them out.

The first hurdle I experienced during the field research phase of my project was *finding* guerrilla veterans to interview. My first two leads actually came by accident. I was at a dinner party with my wife's colleagues, and they asked about my project. I gave them the short answer "I'm writing about guerrilla warfare in the Philippines during World War Two." To my amazement, one lady said she knew two guerrilla veterans, and would pass along my information. I came to learn that she was a physical therapist for the Department of Veterans Affairs, and two of her clients were in fact former guerrillas. In that instance, I found a "gatekeeper" who could vouch for me.

I was also able to locate veterans through two organizations of which I am a member--the American Legion and Veterans of Foreign Wars. One Chicago American Legion Post, Post Number 509, is solely made up of Filipino and Filipino-American veterans. I found that my veteran's status helped immensely, as the Filipino veterans viewed the interviews as conversations between veterans, rather than interviews coming from a graduate student.

As I was searching for veterans, I was also forming my questionnaire (Appendix A). I formulated a four section questionnaire. Section 1 asked for personal information, such as name, date of birth, and military unit. Section 2 utilized a five point Lichert Scale, and asked the veteran their opinion on the Bataan Campaign. My motive was to ascertain whether the veteran's views on the campaign matched the conventional, Americentric history of the campaign.

Section 3 also used the Lichert Scale, and measured the veteran's attitude towards the Imperial Japanese soldiers. Section 4 did not use a Lichert Scale, instead requesting written answers from the veteran. This section asked questions about the veteran's views on the Philippines' revolutionary past; Philippine independence; patriotism; and the decision-making cycle that led the veteran to join the guerrillas.

The questions were purposefully direct, in order to leave the minimal amount of interpretation by the respondent. At the same time, the questionnaire had ample space between questions, so that the veteran could add whatever information he felt appropriate. This "space between" was significant to my research, as financial limitations prohibited my traveling to personally interview each veteran. This technique paid huge dividends, as most of the veterans wrote valuable information in the margins of their questionnaire.

I sent the questionnaire to 30 veterans whose veteran status and address I was able to verify. I received positive responses from 5; a negative response from 1; no response from 22; and 2 veterans who received the questionnaire, but passed away before completion.

Of the five veterans who completed and returned my questionnaire, I was able to interview two in person, and one over the telephone. I corresponded with the last two via US Mail, asking additional questions beyond the original questionnaire. Of the five veterans who agreed to be interviewed, brief profiles follow. Out of respect for the veteran's privacy, only first names are used.

- Third Lieutenant Arcadio of the Philippine Commonwealth Army's 301st Field Artillery Regiment. Arcadio entered military service via the draft. He fought as a heavy artillery officer during the Bataan campaign. He survived the Death March and imprisonment at Camp O'Donnell before release. Arcadio's health was ruined during his time in prison; he did not take part in guerrilla operations. After the war, he rejoined the army, and served as an

Infantry company commander in the re-constituted Philippine Scouts.

- First Sergeant Jose of the Philippine Commonwealth Army's 1st Regular Division was wounded during the retreat to Bataan. He survived the Death March before escaping to the jungle to become a guerrilla. Jose took part in the raid to free American POWs imprisoned at Cabanatuan. After the war, Jose remained in the Philippine Army, fighting again in Korea.

- Corporal Frederico, 45th Infantry Regiment (Philippine Scouts) initially entered the commonwealth army via the draft. Frederico survived the Death March and imprisonment as a POW before becoming a guerrilla. He received the Bronze Star Medal for valor in action for leading a guerrilla raid on a Japanese base in the summer of 1944. He would make the US Army a career, retiring as a Major.

- Corporal Primitivo, 57th Infantry Regiment (Philippine Scouts), received three Purple Heart Medals for being wounded on three separate occasions during the Bataan campaign. Primitivo survived the Death March and imprisonment before becoming a guerrilla.

- Private Domingo, 45th Infantry Regiment (Philippine Scouts), survived the Death March and imprisonment as a POW before becoming a guerrilla. Domingo was awarded the Bronze Star Medal for valor during guerrilla operations. He would make the US Army a career, retiring as a Sergeant First Class.

I was also able to communicate, through correspondence, with two American veterans who had served in the Philippines, and had firsthand knowledge of Filipino guerrillas. The first was John, a field artillery officer in the Philippine Scouts, who fought during the Bataan campaign, and subsequently as a guerrilla leader before escaping to Australia. The second veteran was Salvador, a member of the US Army's 81st Infantry Division, which helped liberate the island of Leyte in the summer of 1945. During that campaign, the 81st Infantry Division was aided by Filipino guerrillas. Both men were able to provide valuable personal insight into the Filipino guerrilla movement.

In each case where I was able to interview the veteran in person, I began the process by speaking with the veteran over the phone, and settling on a date and time to meet. In each case I let the veteran decide the location and time, as I wanted them to be in an environment where they were most comfortable. I utilized two small tape recorders to record the interview: the first utilized micro-cassettes, and the other was digital (they were not used concurrently; the digital recorder was a replacement after the first recorder broke). The tape recorder was to ensure the greatest accuracy of data collection.

I also took notes by hand, so that I would have information for immediate use during the interview. My notes recorded my impressions at the time, and sometimes noted what the veteran *was not* saying. Finally, my hand-written notes listed possible themes for the final book.

Initially, I had planned to conduct the interview in a structured format. However, I immediately learned that trying to structure the interview was the worst possible strategy when dealing with ninety year old veterans. Trying to interject questions, even at times when manners permitted, only served to derail the interview process. So instead, I let the veteran speak at his pace, in whatever direction he felt. I found that this method could sometimes be inefficient, as the conversation would veer wildly off subject—one veteran spent the better half of an hour explaining to me that he was willing to go back to the Philippines to find me a "nice Filipino girl" for a wife. While I was grateful for his kindness, I felt the offer might aggravate my actual wife. Eventually though, I always was able to gain the information needed for my project. By listening with the least amount of questions, I was able to learn what memories were most important to the veterans.

After concluding the interviews, when the information was freshest, I would perform a sort of "after action review." I would listen to the audio recording of the interview while reviewing my notes. I would note anything of interest that I had not noticed during the interview. Usually this would take place in the nearest coffee house, or while sitting in my parked truck. By doing this as soon as the interview was finished, I could really put the interview into the context of what I wanted to portray in my final project, while the information was still fresh in my mind.

Once I returned home, I put the written notes and micro-cassette in a file folder labeled with the veteran's name. Later, when I switched to the digital recorder, I would transfer the interview to my computer. Having the interview on the recorder and the computer provided a measure of redundancy. The veterans' files, micro-cassettes and both recorders were kept locked in a file cabinet in my home.

The biggest research problem I experienced was the advanced age and rough life experiences of my research subjects. The Bataan Campaign had seen the deaths of thousands of Filipinos; the Death March and subsequent imprisonment took the lives of thousands more. Surviving combat, death marches, and guerrilla war is not a recipe for long life, and many guerrilla veterans did not live for very long after the war. When I began my research in 2005, the war had been over for sixty years, and most of the guerrilla veterans were in their eighties. As of this writing, they are all in their nineties. So I consider myself fortunate that I was able to find and interview the five veterans that I did.

A second problem, which I found very interesting, was "fake" guerrillas. In the Filipino culture, being a *guerrillero* during World War Two carries with it a certain status. Though the veterans themselves reject the title, they *are* heroes to the great majority of Filipino society. Though I had not anticipated it when I began my research, there are guerrilla imposters; men who lie about their military service in order to bask in the perceived glory of the World War Two Filipino guerrilla.

Most of these imposters probably would have gone undiscovered had it not been for the Filipino Veteran's Equity Act of 2009. This act, passed by the U.S. Congress and signed by President Obama, provided a one-time $13,000 cash payment to guerrilla veterans who were U.S. citizens, and $9,000 cash payment to guerrilla veterans who were Philippine citizens. In actuality, the cash payment was money the guerrillas were owed as "back pay" for the years they spent fighting in the jungles, while they were on the U.S. government payroll. In order to collect this payment, guerrilla veterans had to provide paperwork showing that they were in fact guerrillas. This caused an interesting rift in the Filipino veterans' community, as the pay-out amounted to a challenge to prove the authenticity of their claims.

One guerrilla veteran I interviewed was former First Sergeant Jose; his adventures are chronicled in the prologue. Jose had made it his personal mission to see that every possible guerrilla veteran received his back pay. Jose related that some of the men he knew, who claimed to be guerrillas, backed away when he tried to help them complete the paperwork necessary to receive the government check. When I asked him why a veteran would not want his back pay, Jose replied that these men were not real guerrillas; they did not want him to delve too deeply into their military past, since they had exaggerated or lied about it. Jose, who I interviewed in his apartment in a heavily Filipino assisted living community, named fellow veterans in his building who were "false guerrillas (his term)." He had told me the names so that I could avoid interviewing them.

Later, I had the opportunity to speak with a "false guerrilla." I was waiting to interview a guerrilla veteran in the Jose Rizal Community Center in Chicago. I had the opportunity to speak with a group of Filipino veterans who were patiently waiting for their American Legion meeting to start. I noticed one man, who remained quiet throughout the conversation, and who stood back from the group. He was wearing a baseball hat with the Philippine Scouts logo on the front. After the group disbanded, this man walked up to me and started telling me how he was a former guerrilla, but he could not get his government check because of "problems with the papers." I made a mental note to try to follow up with this gentleman. When I mentioned the conversation to "my" veteran during the interview, the veteran shook his head and told me he knew the man through their American Legion Post, and that the man was not a guerrilla. My veteran related that all the man's military service had been post-World War Two.

Chapter Four: Relative Deprivation

There are a number of excellent works on political violence, which are indispensable reading for anyone attempting to study the field. In all but one of the works I used, a model was presented. The models proved invaluable, as they allowed the circumstances of the WWII Philippines to be inserted for quick analysis. After studying multiple sources, one proved most useful in my analysis of the Pinoy guerrillas.

Charles and Louise Tilly, advocating the Political Conflict Model, state that political action stems from a reaction to state building. The Political Conflict Model dismisses emotional drive, or lack of economic access. Rather, the Political Conflict Model contains two imperatives for successful revolts: organization and resources (Tilly, 1975). The Tillys' expertise, it is worth noting, is European political movements. Their thesis has some overlap in the Philippines, but for the most part does not fit.

The first imperative in the Political Conflict Model is organization. In this aspect, the Philippines' guerrilla movement does fit the model (to an extent). Much of the historiography, and a lot of US Army records, portray the Filipino guerrillas as a unified force. But in fact, the organization was centralized only inasmuch as the US Army desired it to be. To the US Army's bureaucratic mind, the guerrillas *had* to be centralized, with a defined chain of command. But the distances between the guerrilla bands were often too far for mutual support—even when on the same island. Inter-island cooperation between guerrilla units was barely even contemplated.

Additionally, very few of the guerrilla bands were large. In cities like Manila, or in rural areas like the Luzon plains, guerrilla bands were necessarily small. The local economy could not support large groups of armed warriors. Having smaller groups did not make weaker groups; in fact, quite the opposite. Smaller groups required less of a bureaucracy for administration; a strong-unit leader could manage just fine by leading through force of personality. Many of these small guerrilla units were commanded by former members of the Philippine Commonwealth Army or Philippine Scouts.[2]

In larger units, the leadership was often provided by American military personnel who had escaped the Japanese dragnet. Again, the smaller size was beneficial, as none of the guerrilla leaders in the Philippines during WWII had large-unit command experience. Examples would be Ray Hunt, an American Air Force mechanic, who improvised insurgent warfare on the spot; or John Morrett, a seminary-educated reservist who put his date of ordaining on hold to fight as a field artillery officer. In the cases of Hunt and Morrett, and so many others, guerrilla warfare was an act of improvisation; fitting their prior military experiences into their present circumstances.

The Philippine guerrilla movement lacked resources, at least in the beginning of the war.

---

[2] There were a few high-ranking US Army officers who took to the hills to become guerrillas early in 1942. However, few survived longer than a few months. The bulk of guerrilla leadership was the younger and fitter generation: Lieutenants and Sergeants who assumed command.

Guerrillas fought with whatever they could find; typically machete-like farm tools called *bolos,* or captured Japanese weapons. As the war progressed U.S. Navy submarines were able to bring supplies to some of the *Pinoy* guerrillas. However, the further the guerrilla band was from the coast, the less they received, as they were the end of the logistical tail. Some guerrilla bands, such as the nominally communist *Hukbalahap*, received neither recognition nor supplies from the United States (though they would state that they had picked up such vast quantities of discarded U.S. weapons on Bataan, that they did not need assistance).

Tilly's reliance on access to resources is the main reason I did not rely on the Political Conflict Model to analyze the Filipino guerrilla movement. This is because guerrilla movements, by design, is a means of warfare for the "have nots." Guerrilla movements are popular because they allow the materially weak to effectively fight the mighty.

In contrast to the Tillys' Political Conflict Model, Chalmers Johnson wrote the Value Consensus Model.

The sharpest contrast between the two models is that Johnson's model takes into account human psychology. Johnson proffers that above all other considerations, the collective values of a given society towards their political system will decide whether or not a revolt occurs (Oberschall, 1997). As long as the political power-in-charge rules in such a manner as to not upset the core values of a society, that power will maintain their position. It is analogous to the keel of a sailing ship; as long as the ship stays straight, the boat will operate properly. If the boat lists too far to either side, the ship will capsize. The same applies to the political actor running a particular organization. If the actor rules or legislates in such a manner as to radically change the core values of the masses, the masses will cease to see the political ruler as legitimate. With legitimacy vanished, revolution is often close behind.

Johnson's Value Consensus Model is very applicable to 20th century politics; when I first read his model, the Solidarity movement of 1983 Poland first leapt to mind. However, the Value Consensus Model does not solidly apply to WWII Philippines (It fits quite well to the anti-Marcos "People Power" movement of the 1980's).

During World War II, the *Pinoys* did not have a significant value shift. They remained pro-American and fiercely nationalistic throughout the war. The Philippines does support the Value Consensus Model in that there was not political legitimacy to the occupation government, no matter how hard the Japanese tried. With the notable exception of three individuals: President Quezon, Vice President Osmena and Supreme Court Justice Abad Santos, almost all of the pre-war Philippine Commonwealth politicians served the Japanese. These pre-war politicians formed a government which, on the surface, was pro-Japanese. In reality, each Filipino member of the Japanese occupation government collaborated to different degrees. Some were fiercely anti-Japanese, while others were sycophants. The occupation government lacked legitimacy because the average *Pinoy* knew that, regardless of true feelings, the collaborators were materially benefiting from their service to the Japanese.

Relative Deprivation and the Filipino Guerrilla

Experience

Both the Political Conflict Model and the Value
Consensus Model have some aspects that apply to
World War Two Philippines. But neither model best
covers the Filipino guerrilla experience. The best, most
complete model I have found for explaining the Filipino
guerrilla movement is Ted Robert Gurr's Relative
Deprivation Model. The Relative Deprivation Model,
which has been in use in Political Science for over 60
years, can explain revolutions in terms of the actors'
perceptions of their well-being in relation to those
around them. As Walker and Smith succinctly put it
"people's reactions to objective circumstances depend
on their subjective comparisons (Walker and Smith,
2002).

Gurr's Relative Deprivation construct is explained in
the 1969 Political Science classic "Why Men Rebel."
Gurr's model fleshes out the earlier research of Samuel
Stouffer, who originated the concept of relative
deprivation through research into the attitudes of
World War Two American soldiers. Stouffer's concept

of relative deprivation was rather nebulous inasmuch as he never actually *defined* the term. Stouffer was interested in attitude, specifically the way that American soldiers self-defined deprivation as having more/less than their colleagues. Stouffer's examples include married soldiers feeling they have been deprived of "more" than unmarried soldiers. Another example would be front-line soldiers feeling they were receiving less rations than rear echelon troops, or troops in the Pacific Theatre feeling they had a "tougher war" than soldiers in the European Theatre.

In many cases, Relative Deprivation proved its worth by showing that attitudes were often exactly the opposite of what one would normally think. As an example, Stouffer found that African-American military personnel stationed in the Jim Crow Southern United States were actually *happier* than their African-American counterparts stationed in the North. Stouffer found that African-Americans expected to encounter racism in the South; thus they were not surprised when they found it. Conversely, African-American soldiers stationed in the North expected equality, and were disillusioned when instead they met racism similar to that in the South.

In "Why Men Rebel" Gurr went a step further than Stouffer by creating a model that defined relative deprivation, as well as applying the Relative Deprivation Model to political violence (Gurr, 1970). The Relative Deprivation Model goes beyond the Political Conflict Model and the Value Consensus Model by marrying human psychology to political violence; and it goes beyond Stouffer's research because it can be applied to multiple political violence movements.

The Relative Deprivation Model has certain key components one must understand to utilize the model. First, the Relative Deprivation Model sets aside the earlier works of Weber and Hobbes, which stated that coercion was "the exclusive right of the state." Because Gurr's model rests on individual perception of "what ought" and "what is," non-authoritative violence becomes justified. This dovetails with Laqueur's research into post-WWII guerrilla movements, in which 'legality' of violence is not relevant to the decision to use violence.

Another key component to Relative Deprivation is the presence of rational choice. Rational choice is the cornerstone of the Relative Deprivation Model (if not for most of Social Science). Rational choice is the assumption that any given actor is making consistent choices, based on available data, with the ultimate goal of maximizing his or her net benefit. This is especially important in relative deprivation-based political violence studies, since the violence erupts when net benefit does not meet the expectations of the actors.

The Relative Deprivation Model relies on the relationship between *value expectations* and *value capabilities* (Gurr, 1970). "Value expectations" refers to the physical goods and emotional conditions that the actor believes are deserved. "Value capabilities" refers to the goods and conditions that the actor feels are achievable. As stated earlier, value expectations are the "ought" and value capabilities are the "is." When the discrepancy between rising value expectations and falling value capabilities becomes too great across society, conditions exist for possible political violence.

Gurr describes the moment-of-action for political violence movements utilizing a number of different hypotheses. In each hypothesis, either the value expectation rises beyond a level sustainable by value capability; or value capability plummets below the range of value expectation. In some cases, value expectation rises *and* value capability plummets. Gurr's hypothesis VE.1 is the hypothesis that best replicates the path to Filipino guerrilla warfare. In my research notes, I referred to this hypothesis as the "conversion hypothesis" after some of the key words in Gurr's explanation. In the conversion hypothesis, expectations positively spike through "symbolic exposure to a new mode of life." Capabilities can either: A) stay the same; B) rise; C) plummet; or D) positively spike in equal parts to expectations (an almost impossible scenario). In the case of the Philippine guerrilla movement, the conversion hypothesis fits because the Philippines has both the sharp spike in value expectations, followed shortly by a sharp decline in value capabilities (Gurr, 1970).

The positive spike was provided by the 1934 Tydings-McDuffie Act. As will be explained later,

Tydings-McDuffie paved the way for Philippine independence. After nearly 40 years of American presence in the islands, the Pinoys could finally see a future in which they ruled themselves. Thus, the value expectations of the Filipinos justifiably spiked. They believed that President Roosevelt and the US Congress would honor Tydings-McDuffie, and that they would be free.

At the same time, value capabilities were slowly rising. The Philippines was able to develop industry and infrastructure, while maintaining their agricultural production. American style democracy had flourished, and the *Pinoys* believed in the sanctity of voting. They were sending their children to quality public schools, and had access to university educations. Additionally important, neither the spike of expectation, nor the slow rise of capabilities altered the basic view the Filipinos had of their world.

Factually, it would have been impossible for value capabilities to spike in equal measures with value expectations—for the simple reason that capabilities exist in the real world, while expectations exist in the mind. The Filipinos understood this, so the disparity did not move them towards political violence. Besides, knowing that they were going to gain control of their capabilities far outweighed the current level of tangibles.

The drop in value capabilities occurred almost immediately upon Japanese invasion. When in graphic form, the Philippine example of the conversion hypothesis would look like a street that intersects in a side-ways "T." The left, or high road, would represent the value expectation; the right, or low road, the value capability.

Much of the reason for the drop in value capability has already been mentioned, with the destruction of the metropolitan Manila area, and the massive prisoner deaths at the hands of the Japanese Army. To add to that, the Japanese Army looted the Philippine treasury, sending the gold and silver reserves back to Japan. They also destroyed the local economy by confiscating large amounts of the rice crop. At the same time, the Japanese initiated a puppet government which recklessly substituted a cotton-based economy for the traditional rice-based agricultural economy. That being said, one must analyze why this is the tipping point in the *Pinoys'* move to guerrilla warfare.

Gurr noted that dissatisfaction exists in all societies, and does not necessarily lead to political violence. Many countries were conquered during World War Two, and few had the ferocious guerrilla movement of the Philippines. Numerous factors that could lead to political violence lived in the chasm between value expectations and value capabilities. Gurr lists these factors as: legitimacy of the state; previous success of political violence movements; symbolic appeals to violence; the state's response to deprivation; and the utility of violence in closing the gap between capabilities and expectations (Gurr, 1970). If the devil is in the details, than this is where one will find the impetus for the guerrilla movement in the Philippines.

A) *Legitimacy of the State:*

First, there was absolutely no legitimacy in the Japanese puppet government. While a small minority of Filipinos believed Japanese rule was preferable to

American rule, that minority never had real access to power. The overwhelming majority of Filipinos believed that the Japanese sanctioned government was nothing but a reign of terror. The legitimacy of the Japanese puppet government was eroded by the "puppets" themselves, many of whom were secret supporters of the guerrillas. Further erosion came about through assassinations of puppet politicians. The most famous of these was the attempted assassination of Japanese-backed President Jose Laurel, who was shot three times in the chest while playing golf.[3] Though he lived, the Laurel shooting proved to the Japanese that their puppets could be attacked at the guerrillas' will.

B) Previous Success in Political Violence Movements:

As stated in the introduction, the *Pinoys* were no strangers to insurgent movements. Most of their national heroes are *guerrilleros.* Jose Rizal and Andres

---

[3] Ironically, Jose Laurel was a supporter of the guerrillas. When his would-be assassin was captured by the Japanese Secret Police (Kempetei), Laurel refused to identify the man, saying he was not the assassin. A decade later, Laurel was elected to the Philippine Senate. Knowing he needed a bodyguard, Laurel hired the former guerrilla-hitman.

Bonifacio were martyrs for the cause of independence: Rizal against the Spanish and Bonifacio against the Americans. At the time of the Japanese invasion, many anti-American *guerrilleros* were still alive and venerated as heroes (the fact that they fought losing battles was irrelevant to the *guerrilleros*). In Philippine culture, in which elder respect is sacred, aged anti-American guerrillas essentially "blessed" the anti-Japanese guerrilla movement. In fact, many former anti-American guerrillas came out of retirement to help fight the Japanese.

C) *The State's response to deprivation:*

How the Japanese responded to deprivation is also a key factor on the road to political violence. The Japanese occupation appeared schizophrenic to the *Pinoys*, because there was no unified structure to the Japanese. By order of the Meiji constitution, the Imperial Japanese Army and Navy were independent of civil authority; they answered directly to the Emperor. In contrast, the Japanese Foreign Ministry answered to the Prime Minister. Being diplomats by profession, the Foreign Ministry attempted to win the loyalty of the

Filipino people. The Imperial Japanese Army, which was responsible for the physical occupation of the Philippines, viewed the Filipinos as racially inferior and treated them as such. This divergent attitude would lead to Filipino frustration, as any peaceful act by the Foreign Ministry was almost immediately negated by the violence of the Imperial Japanese Army.

The treatment of Filipino prisoners-of-war during the Bataan Death March, and their subsequent imprisonment, led many Filipino soldiers to the guerrillas' cause. With the exception of Third Lieutenant Arcadio (who could not join the guerrillas due to health ruined during imprisonment), all the veterans I interviewed became resolved to be guerrillas because they lost friends during the Death March. It was as if their soldiers' minds could accept seeing their comrades die in battle, but could not accept watching these same comrades murdered as prisoners. They did not see their desire to continue fighting as revenge; rather they saw it as the soldier's duty to resist at all costs—Private Primitivo even referred to his stint as a *guerrillero* as returning "back to regular service."

D) *Symbolic appeals to violence*:

The United States was instrumental in providing the symbolic call to violence. "Radio Free Philippines" beamed radio signals to the Philippines from their home base in San Francisco, California. Filipinos were able to hear addresses from President Quezon, President Roosevelt, and General MacArthur. American submarines brought food, ammunition and supplies to the Filipino resistance. Among the supplies was candy bars, pencils, stationary and postage stamps emblazoned with MacArthur's iconic statement "I shall return." The postage stamps were so wildly popular that the Japanese occupation forces could not stop their usage; instead the post office processed them as usual. Submarines also brought to the Philippines gold, which was stored away to purchase supplies. Guerrilla groups even began printing their own currency, which was backed by the American gold. Often, the guerrilla currency featured portraits of FDR and MacArthur. Much like the postage stamps, the guerrilla money was preferred to the Japanese occupation currency, which Lieutenant Arcadio and First Sergeant Jose both derisively called "Mickey Mouse money." Candy bars, stamps, machine guns, special currency; it was all designed to keep the guerrillas fighting, while serving as a reminder that America would return.

D) *Utility of Violence*:

For the *Pinoys*, utility of violence is easy to explain, inasmuch as they had no other option. Not only had they been defeated in battle, and massacred during the Bataan Death March, but after their imprisonment, murder was all around them. The Japanese response to most guerrilla operations is what the Filipinos called "the *Zona*." Even after 70 years, when I brought up the subject of the *Zona* to veterans, they would always get a sad, far off look in their eyes. The *Zona* began with the Japanese capturing a Filipino—guerrilla or not, no matter—and torturing said Filipino until he agreed to provide names of "other" guerrillas. The Japanese would then escort the prisoner to his village, with a flour sack or a basket over his head so he could not be identified. The occupants of the village would be rounded up, and the prisoner would point out the supposed members of the guerrillas. Those who were identified would be killed on the spot. The damage was not only in the loss of life; it was also psychological, as the villagers would never know who was behind the mask.

With instances like this, it is no wonder that the *guerrilleros* felt they had no choice but to resort to violence. There was no outlet for peaceful discussion; no way for the guerrillas to negotiate. With so much violence being done to them, they felt that they had no recourse but to answer violence with violence. For a country with deeply held Christian values, the move to violence was not an easy one. But circumstances were such that violence was one of two available choices, with the other being capitulation. When they turned to violence, it was often extreme. Corporal Primitivo, who fought as a guerrilla in Batangas Province, related matter-of-factly how they would behead the bodies of Japanese soldiers killed in combat, as a warning to others.

Walang Hiya

For the veterans I interviewed, the transition to guerrilla was particularly bitter. These men had carried the responsibility of defending the Philippines from invaders, and had failed. Despite their heroic attempt to defend Luzon, nothing could change the unbearable fact that *they* had lost their country. The results of their failure were all around them: in the confiscation of the rice crop; their children were forced to learn Japanese in school; they were forced to bow to every Japanese soldier they passed on the street. Every guerrilla veteran I interviewed had internalized this loss.

One soldier I interviewed, Corporal Primitivo, still harbored ill-will towards the Japanese for their treatment of the Filipinos. After twenty years as a professional soldier, and sixty-five years after victory in World War Two, Primitivo still burned at having lost his home to the Japanese. In response to the statement: "I still cannot forgive the Japanese for invading the Philippines," Primitivo unequivocally agreed.

Any soldier would be bothered by defeat, but for the Filipinos, shame was a mixture of their Catholic guilt (94% of Filipinos are Christian) mixed with a particularly Filipino concept called *walang hiya*. *Walang hiya* translates as "much shame," but carries a deeper meaning. To feel *walang hiya* is to know that one has failed in one's obligation to others. No guerrilla veteran I spoke to directly mentioned *walang hiya*; it is always a taboo topic in polite conversation. But when describing their feelings and actions, these aged former guerrillas always defined *walang hiya*. First Sergeant Jose would later take part in a desperate raid to free American POWs; Frederico would lead a raid on a Japanese fort; Domingo beheaded the Japanese invaders. It is easy to see that the motivation for their brave actions was directly tied to *walang hiya*, and the need to expiate it.

Chapter Five: World War II on Luzon

Pre-War Philippines Politics

Philippine history before the Americans is best represented by a nearly eternal struggle between Filipino insurgent groups and various outside invaders. In fact, the guerrillas of World War Two were heirs to a legacy of political violence. Before the Filipino's recorded history, they were fighting invaders from mainland China and Malaysia; the outcomes of these campaigns are recorded in tribal lore. The tribal leader Lapu-Lapu and his warriors killed Magellan, and sent his despondent crew back to Spain. In this small victory, Lapu-Lapu placed the Philippines into the European consciousness. Despite his victory, the Spanish returned, and dominated the islands for three hundred years, and named the islands after their king.

The Spanish strategy was to dominate the island through a small oligarchy, rather than wholesale settlement. Over time, this management style created a stratified society. At the top of the chain were the "pure-blood" Spaniards. By the late 19th century, the nadir of the Spanish Empire in the Philippines, these pure bloods were generations deep in the Philippines. Many of them never stepped foot on Spain, instead living their lives in service to the notion of Spain.

Directly below the Spanish were the Illustrados, a term which originally applied to mixed heritage Filipino-Spaniards. By the mid-1800's Illustrado commonly meant educated Filipinos (both male and female). The Illustrados quickly realized that despite their education and talent, they would never be allowed access to political power. This realization caused a societal schism between Illustrados who wanted violent revolt, and Illustrados who were unwilling to gamble their status in a bid for freedom.

The pro-revolutionary *Illustrados* would join a middle-class movement called the *Katipunan*, a secret society that advocated the defeat of the Spanish empire, with the ultimate goal of creating an American-style republic. The *Katipunan* naturally drew the third member of their stratified society: the Filipino masses. The vast majority of Filipinos lived in small *barrios,* farming small plots of land and tied to one another through kinship. Though the farmers may not have worried about what happened in far-off Manila, they were more than concerned by the Spanish-levied heavy taxes. The Katipunan would tap into peasant discontent, as well as the discontent of the metropolitan-Manila industrial workers. Such it was that the urban poor, the rural poor, and the nascent Filipino middle class would unite in a nationalist movement worth fighting for.

Ironically, the Filipino dream of an American style-republic would have to wait because of American intervention. The Katipunan would defeat the Spanish on battlefields across Luzon, and the movement would begin to spread to other islands in the Philippine archipelago. But just as the Katipunan were poised to take Manila, the United States Army arrived. Having "won" the Philippines as spoils in the Spanish-American War, the United States had no intention of giving the Pinoys their freedom (Aguinaldo, 2010). The American forces, under the command of Civil War hero General Arthur MacArthur, handily crushed the Katipunan. With the Philippines subjugated—again—the US set out to recreate the Philippines as a "little America" (McKinley, 2006).

Though the crushing of the Katipunan had been brutal, the occupation was the exact opposite. In fact, it is within the framework of the occupation that the US won the loyalty of the Filipino people. The occupying US Army brought with it an American culture that the Filipinos were quick to embrace. American statesmen were sent to the Philippines to construct a political bureaucracy, and to train Filipino leaders. American religious institutions sent missions to the Philippines, and opened public schools. Of these three influences, the public school system had the most impact. Just like in the US public school system, the purpose of the Philippine public school system was to instill appreciation of American civic virtues. This fusion worked perfectly, and many of America's biggest supporters in the Philippines were former Katipuneros. This contradiction would directly benefit the guerrilla cause during the Japanese occupation, as the die-hard pro-American Filipinos would become the most strident anti-Japanese fighters.

The Tydings-McDuffie Act of 1934

In 1934, the United States legislature passed a significant bill sponsored by Senators Millard Tydings (R-MD) and John McDuffie (D-AL). The Tydings-McDuffie Act set the stage for Philippine independence. The bill restructured the Philippines as a commonwealth of the United States. The Philippines would hold elections for President and Vice President, as well as nominate members for a constitutional convention. The Philippine Commonwealth would also structure its own armed forces. But what the Filipinos liked the best was that the date of July 4th, 1946 would be Philippine Independence Day (Pabico, 2006).

After Tydings-McDuffie passed the US Congress, and was signed by President Roosevelt, it had to be ratified by the Philippine National Assembly. This was done immediately. Under the leadership of long-time Filipino politician Jose Yulo, the constitutional convention began writing an American style constitution.

There were two important facets to the Filipino commonwealth structure. First, all decisions of the

Philippine Commonwealth had to be approved by the United States, via an American administrator called a "High Commissioner." The High Commissioner position was filled by career diplomats; usually long-service ambassadors. The purpose of the High Commissioner was to ensure that Filipino legislation was favorable to the US.

Secondly, the Philippines never developed a two-party system. Instead, there were multiple parties—often four or six at a time. In this plurality, the Nacionalista Party was able to consolidate power, and became an oligarchy. The Nacionalista Party contained the two most powerful Filipino politicians of the first half of the twentieth century: President Manuel Quezon and Vice President Sergio Osmena. Quezon was a former Katipunero who had made the transition from guerrilla to politician, and was dying by inches of tuberculosis. Osmena, a Filipino of Chinese ancestry, was a career politician who had been the Philippines' first Speaker of the National Assembly, and had barely lost the presidential election to Quezon. Though both were of the same Nacionalista party, they were also rivals who had worked to undermine each other at various times.

Such it was that, with a world war approaching from the north, the Philippines were governed by two men who did not trust each other, and lacked complete decision making power.

The Philippine Commonwealth Military

To defend the Philippines, President Quezon needed a military. The problem was the lack of Filipino soldiers available to *build* an army. Through a decades old transfer program, each West Point class featured a Filipino national. By 1935, this resulted in only a dozen trained Filipino officers. But with no Filipino Army to command, these trained officers lacked the practical experience necessary to create an armed force from the ground-up. For this, Quezon turned to the only man he felt *could* create an army: General Douglas MacArthur.

General Douglas MacArthur was the son of General Arthur MacArthur, the legendary Civil War-veteran who had finally defeated the Katipunan revolution.

Graduating West Point in 1903, Douglas MacArthur had just missed campaigning against the Katipunan. While stationed in the Philippines, he fell in love with the country and its people. He would become friends with most of the Filipino politicians, and a firm friend of Manuel Quezon (MacArthur, 1964).

In 1935, Douglas MacArthur was ending his tour as Army Chief of Staff, the highest position in the US Army. MacArthur was still young, but was faced with a quandary: since he had made it to the top of the army food chain, he now had nowhere to go but down. Any army assignment he accepted would, in effect, be a demotion. While he was mulling over his career choices, MacArthur was approached by President Quezon with an offer: to become Chief of Staff of the Philippine Commonwealth Army. Quezon promised MacArthur a free hand, with the power to develop the Commonwealth Army however he saw fit. MacArthur accepted the offer, with one change: ever the dramatist, MacArthur demanded that his title not be "General," but "Field Marshal."

MacArthur's plan was to form an army similar to Switzerland's: a system in which all adult males are army reservists, buttressed by a small clique of full-time soldiers. Finland had successfully used this system, mobilizing their reservists to great effect against the Soviet Union in 1940. The main draw of this system was twofold: the maximum amount of soldiers could be trained without upsetting the Filipino economy. Second, this was the least expensive military MacArthur could build—an important factor for the cash strapped Philippines.

In the Philippine system, the professional core of the army would be the 1st Regular Division; this is the division in which First Sergeant Jose served. Jose's company, M Company, 3/1st Infantry Regiment, was a heavy weapons company, with the wartime mission of providing accurate machine gun fire. However, their peacetime role was to be the trainers for the incoming reservists. Each spring, male Filipinos would receive their draft notice, with orders to report to military training camps throughout the islands.

As the soldiers arrived at the camps, they heard many strange languages for the first time. There were over a hundred different dialects in the Philippines. A 1935 Commonwealth Act adopted *Tagalog* as the official language of the Philippines. However, *Tagalog* was the dialect of Manila and the surrounding provinces; the language of the educated politicians. *Tagalog*, simplified and renamed *Pilipino*, still had not reached most of the 7,000 islands of the Philippines. The 1935 decree did not solve the Army's problem: soldiers couldn't communicate with their Sergeants; Sergeants couldn't communicate with their officers. The Army initially tried to group the men by dialect, but the plan failed (though a few companies, made up of headhunters from Ilo Ilo, would prove ferocious fighters). Most of the officers, who by necessity needed to be educated, only spoke *Tagalog*. The issue was never resolved, and the Philippine Commonwealth Army would walk into combat often lacking the ability to communicate simple needs.

The camps were simple affairs composed of bamboo buildings with nipa-palm roofs. Incoming soldiers were issued khaki short sleeved shirts and shorts. For footwear, they were issued low-topped tennis shoes. Because steel helmets were expensive, the men were issued helmets made from shellacked coconut leaves, called *guinit* helmets. The helmets offered no protection from bullets or explosions, and they deteriorated quickly in the tropic heat. At least they gave the soldiers uniformity. Equipment was also in short supply. Soldiers performed close order drill and the manual of arms carrying bamboo sticks as substitute rifles (Jose, 1992).

One of these new recruits was Frederico. Frederico was a student when he was drafted in 1939. He liked military service, but was not impressed by the low pay and poor equipment of the Philippine Commonwealth Army. Frederico, who hoped to make a career in the service, applied for a transfer out of the Commonwealth Army, and into an elite US Army unit called the Philippine Scouts.

While new Private Frederico burned to get out of the Commonwealth Army and into the Scouts, MacArthur traveled to Washington, D.C., using his personal influence to purchase what surplus US equipment was available. The United States, still deep in the Great Depression, hadn't invested in their military, either. Armored units painted the word "tank" on the sides of trucks, and simulated war games. Infantry soldiers, for so long proud of their marksmanship skills, were severely limited in the amount of ammunition they were allowed to fire.

MacArthur was able to purchase large stocks of the Model 1917 Rifle, the main U.S. battle rifle of World War One. After they were shipped to the Philippines and issued to soldiers, it was discovered that the rifles were too long for the shorter Filipinos (Jose, 1992). The inability to properly aim the rifles would vastly degrade their accuracy. After the Japanese invaded, the Filipinos learned that the extractors on their rifles were brittle from age. The extractor, which pulls the spent cartridge out of the rifle's breach, would snap off, leaving the brass cartridge stuck in the throat of the rifle. Filipino riflemen would take to carrying thin bamboo sticks. After each shot, they would jam the bamboo down the barrel of their antiquated rifles, and pop the cartridge out. This left the Filipino soldiers without the ability to fire the 8 to 10 aimed rounds a minute expected of their rifles.

General MacArthur was also able to obtain field artillery, in the form of old British and American howitzers. Heavy and ungainly, most lacked sites and fire direction equipment. The net result was that the artillery had to be fired by "direct lay." This meant the gunners would have to visually see the enemy, and point the cannon by sight while estimating distance to the enemy. On the verge of a world war, the Philippine army was firing their cannons in the same manner as Napoleon.

As career sergeants like First Sergeant Jose attempted to train new recruits like Frederico, Third Lieutenant Arcadio arrived at the 301st Field Artillery. A recent college graduate with a degree in forestry, Arcadio was in the process of taking civil service tests when his draft notice arrived. The Commonwealth Army saw that he had a university education, and shipped him off for field artillery officer's training. The Philippine Commonwealth Army made a good choice by putting Arcadio in command; he was a natural leader who easily gained the respect of his troops.

Third Lieutenant Arcadio's training was fast but thorough. It had to be, as he would end up being the most thoroughly trained soldier in his battery. He was also lucky: the 301st Field Artillery Regiment was armed with French 155 millimeter cannons called "Grande Puissance Filloux." The largest field artillery available in the Philippines, they were called "Long Toms" by the artillerymen. The Long Tom 155mm cannons could hurl a large shell 14 kilometers—farther than any cannon the Japanese would bring to the Philippines.

The Philippine Scouts

The defense of the Philippines would hinge on MacArthur's commonwealth army. But the *backbone* of the defense would be provided by an elite Filipino-American unit called the Philippine Scouts. The Philippine Scouts was a group of soldiers that dated back to the Philippine-American War. They were originally Filipinos who chose to side with the US Army against the insurgent forces of Emilio Aguinaldo. In fact, it was a group of Philippine Scouts, led by American Army Colonel Frederick Funston, which captured Aguinaldo, thereby bringing the Filipino-American war to an end. The scouts were even featured as an exhibit at the 1904 World's Fair in St. Louis.

In the years after the Filipino-American War, the Philippine Scouts were officially adopted into the United States Army as "The Philippine Division (Philippine Scouts)." Each scout unit carried the initials "PS" after its name, to differentiate them from white US Army units (Stanton, 2006). Composed of American officers and Filipino enlisted men, they were a crack unit, renowned for their discipline and marksmanship skills. The Division was made up of three Infantry regiments (one of which was all white), four Field Artillery regiments and support troops. There were also Coast Artillery units and one Cavalry regiment.

Service in the Philippine Scouts was considered a great honor; one did not merely enlist in the scouts.

Instead, there was a sort of apprenticeship program, where prospective scouts would hang around the unit they wished to join. In many cases, these prospects were "sons of the unit" who were trying to follow in their fathers' paths (Lapham, 1996). These prospective scouts would perform menial tasks, such as cleaning the barracks or unit equipment—all while receiving no pay.

In return for their labor, the prospective recruits would be taught basic military skills by the units' Sergeants and Corporals. One of these Corporals was Primitivo, who had enlisted in 1939. While stationed at Fort McKinley, near Manila, he had soldiered hard and been promoted to Corporal in the headquarters of the 57th Infantry (PS). In the 57th Infantry's sister regiment, the 45th Infantry (PS), Corporal Frederico was also training troops. Frederico wanted to make the Army a career, and had transferred to the Scouts from the commonwealth troops. He was promoted to Corporal in April of 1941. Both Frederico and Primitivo would find their leadership skills sorely tested on Bataan.

The Sergeants and Corporals would observe the would-be recruits, to ensure they had the proper temperament for Army life. If an opening in the unit occurred, the Sergeants would have a ready supply of recruits, who had already received some military training. The system worked well, as the scouts were able to pick the best-of-the-best. In once instance, an Infantry rifle company had twenty openings; the commander had so many applicants that he was able to pick twenty college educated men (at a time when 74% of US Army enlisted men did not have high school diplomas). Sterling behavior was the standard, as infractions could result in the soldier being discharged from the unit. Lieutenant John, a white officer who commanded a scout field artillery battery, wrote me that he never saw or heard of any of his scouts drinking alcoholic beverages.

Twenty or thirty year careers were the norm, as no one ever wanted to leave the Scouts (War Department Circular No. 41, 1931). Even in retirement, the scouts never strayed too far from their beloved army—most retired scouts lived in *barrios* near their former posts. When the Japanese landed in December, 1941, many retired scouts returned to their old units, and fought for no pay.

Unlike the Commonwealth Army, which suffered from low pay and non-existent equipment, the Scouts belonged to the US Army, and were outfitted exactly the same as white American army units. They received well made uniforms and equipment, including steel helmets and stout leather boots. They were fed typical US Army rations and received government provided medical care. Their vehicles were new, and their cavalry received the highest quality horses available. Because the scouts were a showcase unit, they were the first to receive the M1 Garand, a rapid firing semi-automatic rifle. Corporal Primitivo, who fought up and down the Bataan Peninsula with the 57th Infantry (PS), had absolute faith in the dependability of his Garand rifle. When the time came, the Scouts would shock the Imperial Japanese Army with their high rates of accurate fire.

Because most troops in the scouts served until retirement, promotions were rare. Scouts averaged six years of service before they received their first promotion to Private First Class. When World War Two broke out, these long-service scouts would prove a godsend to the Philippines. Many would be detached to serve as cadre in the Philippine Commonwealth Army, to provide a steadying influence among the poorly trained draftees. The scouts also provided a psychological edge to the Philippine Commonwealth Army, as the sight of the well disciplined scouts, marching relentlessly towards the enemy, would buoy the scared Commonwealth soldiers. And even later, when all seemed lost, everyone looked to the Philippine Scouts to shore up the lines. This they would do, time after time, much to the consternation of the Imperial Japanese Army.

The Bataan Campaign

In 1941, with war on the horizon, the US Army recalled MacArthur to active duty as a Lieutenant General in the US Army. He was given command of USAFFE: US Armed Forces, Far East. Despite the change, he was still fulfilling the same task: to defend the Philippines from Japanese invasion. In a process similar to the call-up of the National Guard, the

Philippine Commonwealth Army was adopted into the US Army. Commonwealth soldiers swore an oath of allegiance to the United States.

The adoption of the Philippine Commonwealth Army was not merely a semantic ploy; it had a real-world goal. As "Commonwealth" forces, each unit had American officers and senior non-commissioned officers assigned as advisers. Once they were incorporated into the US Army, the American advisers—most of whom were combat veterans of World War One—could assert a greater degree of decision making.

The Philippines were attacked on the eighth of December, 1941 (actually the same day as the Pearl Harbor attack, but technically different because of the International Date Line). The initial attack on the Philippines was via the Japanese Army's air wing; fast silver fighters and bombers that swooped out of the sky and destroyed the Filipino-American military bases.

The Philippine defenders were taken completely by surprise. First Sergeant Jose was marching his soldiers to the dining facility for lunch when he saw silver airplanes flying in the sky. It was not until the planes began to bomb and strafe his formation that he realized they were Japanese. Jose ordered his men to jump into drainage ditches for safety. Despite his quick actions, he was wounded in the arm and shoulder by shrapnel from an exploding bomb.

At Clark Air Field, near Manila, the US Army Air Force had parked their planes wingtip to wingtip, as it was easier to guard. It was also easier for them to be strafed by enemy warplanes. In one raid, the Japanese air force was able to destroy almost every plane the Americans and Filipinos had. Shortly after the raid, the Army Air Force would order its heavy bombers, the B-17's, to leave Luzon for Mindanao (and later for Australia). The few fighter planes to survive the onslaught, mostly P-40 Warhawks, would be used for reconnaissance. Never during the Bataan campaign would the Japanese supremacy in the air be challenged.

At the same time, the US Navy decided that their port at Subic Bay, north of Manila, was indefensible.

With the exception of a few small patrol boats and maintenance craft that could not make the ocean voyage to Australia, the U.S. Navy left the Philippines. The Japanese had not even stepped foot in the Philippines, yet the defending forces were already without a navy and air force.

Fort McKinley, in the suburbs of Manila, was the main US Army garrison in the Philippines. It was at McKinley that the 45th and 57th Philippine Scout Infantry regiments were stationed. They too were taken by surprise, when the silver Japanese fighters flew over. Unlike the commonwealth troops, the Scouts reacted quicker. First-line leaders like Corporals Primitivo and Frederico rounded up their troops, double-checked their equipment, and prepared them to march off to war.

One of the scouts preparing for war was Private Domingo. Originally from the mountainous northern area of Luzon, Domingo was a member of E Company, Second Battalion of the 45th Infantry (PS). He had spent two years in college before leaving to join the Scouts. Domingo had a deep love of America and a fierce pride in all things Filipino. Private Domingo's pride would sustain him through the three desperate years when he returned to northern Luzon to fight in the guerrilla 11th Infantry.

In the 57th Infantry (PS), the soldiers received a strange order: to shave their heads. The soldiers were initially surprised by such an odd order, until the Sergeants explained that they would be taking to the field, and crew cuts would cut down on incidents of lice. After the Scouts had shaved their heads, they marveled at their burr-cuts while pointing and laughing at each other (Olson, 1991).

As the Scout's Non-Commissioned Officers harangued, and the Privates shaved their heads, the US Army dusted off their antiquated war plans. In the inter-war years, the US military had developed a series of contingency plans in case war erupted. The plans were collectively known as Rainbow 5, and dealt with almost every possible wartime scenario, with each combat theatre assigned a color (Morton, 1953).

The Rainbow plan to defend the Philippines was entitled War Plan Orange 3. Written in part by a then-obscure Major named Dwight Eisenhower, Orange was based on certain fundamental assumptions. First, Orange assumed (correctly, as it turned out) that the Philippines would be invaded by Japan. It also correctly assumed that the campaign for the Philippines would hinge on the Philippines' main island of Luzon, because Luzon contained the metropolitan Manila area. As such, no plan was conceived to defend the Philippines per se, just Luzon.

However, the next two assumptions in the Orange plan doomed the Philippines. First, Orange assumed that the US would only be fighting Japan; the plan did not conceive of a second world war. Unlike the paper plan, reality found the United States in a multiple theatre war. As such, President Roosevelt pledged the U.S. to fight a "Germany first" campaign. The critical troops and supplies urgently needed in the Philippines were instead, sent to Europe. Orange also assumed that the US Navy would be able to ferry troops and supplies to the Philippines to keep the islands from falling. With the Pacific Fleet under water at Pearl Harbor, there was no way the navy could accomplish their part of War Plan Orange 3.

War Plan Orange 3 had no back-up; no flexible answer to the incorrect assumptions. Thus the combined Filipino-American forces were forced to fight according to a fantasy plan which from the start was strategically impossible. The Army's portion of Orange was to pull all available forces onto the Bataan peninsula, a finger of land that helped form Manila Bay. There they would dig in and fight a delaying action.

The army would also occupy a number of small islands near the mouth of Manila Bay; the most important being the island of Corregidor. Orange stated that the Bataan forces only needed to hold out for six months, before reinforcements arrive. But as one can see, War Plan Orange was already moot. Reinforcements would not arrive in six months, but in three years. Bordering Manila Bay on the northwest side, the Bataan peninsula was one of the least settled places on Luzon. It was a strategically important area because Bataan and Corregidor would block Japanese use of the deep-water port and modern docks of Manila. MacArthur would later refer to Corregidor as the "cork" that stoppers the "bottle" of Manila (Whitman, 1990).

As a peninsula, Bataan was favorable for defense because it allowed the Army to anchor their left flank on the steep banks of the South China Sea, and their right flank on Manila Bay. Bataan was covered with thick jungle, and had a (theoretically) impenetrable mountain range running down its center. The western coastline was rocky, and thought unsuitable for amphibious assaults (Whitman, 1990). There was one all-weather road that ran in a "U" shape down the east coast of the peninsula to the town of Mariveles, where it then climbed back up the west coast. Though it was one road, it was referred to as the "West Road" or "East Road" as if it were two roads. There was only one road running laterally across the peninsula, linking the East and West Road. This lateral road ran from the small town of Bagac on the west coast to Pilar on the east coast.

For all it had going for it, there were two principal military drawbacks to the Bataan peninsula. First, Bataan was the most malaria-prone area on all of

Luzon, a fact that would prove heartbreaking to the troops assigned there.

Second, though War Plan Orange 3 had been conceived with MacArthur's input, he no longer believed in it. After fifteen years of planning for Orange, and stockpiling rations, ammunition and medical supplies in dumps on Bataan, MacArthur changed the plan. He decided it would be bad for morale for the Philippine-American forces to dig in on Bataan and wait for help. Instead, he ordered his units to deploy across north and central Luzon to defend the beaches against the inevitable Japanese invasion.

This redeployment played havoc on the logistical system; the supplies that had been carefully stocked on Bataan had to be brought out and distributed to units all over Bataan. The 12th Quartermaster Regiment (Philippine Scouts), responsible for supplying the Philippine Scouts, used borrowed city buses and *carabao* carts get supplies to the troops. As their supply columns snaked up and down the clogged roads of Luzon, they were ceaselessly attacked by Japanese bombers and fighters. Half of the 12th Quartermasters would become casualties during the Bataan campaign. The only member of the 12th Quartermaster Regiment that I could find declined to be interviewed for this research, as the memories were still too hard to take.

In other instances, issues with supply would be laughable had they not led to so much human suffering. One U.S. Army Quartermaster Lieutenant Colonel found a Japanese-owned warehouse that was filled with canned food. He contacted MacArthur's headquarters, with a request for extra supply trucks. The Quartermaster was told that, because the food was private property, it was to be left alone. When the Quartermaster objected, repeating that the food was owned by members of the enemy country, he was threatened with court martial. The Quartermaster left the warehouse empty handed. In another instance, Filipino troops attempted to bring stocks of rice along when they retreated towards Bataan. They were stopped, since it was illegal under Commonwealth law to bring rice from one province into another. In part, it was actions like these that ensured that the Filipino-American troops would starve on Bataan.

As part of the strategic redeployment, the 1st Regular Division of the Commonwealth Army took up positions north of Manila, at Lingayan Gulf. MacArthur had correctly identified Lingayan Gulf as the best place on Luzon for the Japanese to land; they did land there, on the December tenth, 1941. A second Japanese assault force landed near the city of Aparri a few days later. The Japanese soldiers quickly overran the 1st Regular Division. Among the Filipino troops in action was First Sergeant Jose, who killed the sword-wielding Japanese officer. That firefight would be a short-lived victory, as the successful Japanese landing necessitated the first of too many Filipino-American retreats.

When the Philippine Commonwealth Army had to retreat, they did so grudgingly. In one instance, the field artillery battery of the 31st Philippine Commonwealth Division was not notified that the division was in retreat. The gunners, lacking any other orders, spent two days alone on Luzon plains, pouring cannon fire directly into the Japanese (Whitman, 1990). The 31st's divisional commander, Brigadier

General Clifford Bluemel, had to send a staff member to escort the 31st Artillery off the line.

Despite the often staunch defense of the Philippine Commonwealth Army, they continued to be pushed back. The retreat would get worse in the last week of December, when more Japanese forces landed south of Manila at Lamon Bay. The Japanese plan was to catch the Filipino-American forces in a pincer movement. MacArthur realized his army could not stop the Japanese on the beaches, and invoked War Plan Orange 3 on December twenty-third.

The initiation of Orange 3 affected MacArthur personally, as he would literally be abandoning his home in Manila. He relocated his headquarters across the bay to Corregidor, the fortified island blocking Manila Bay. Shaped roughly like a tadpole, Corregidor bristled with large-caliber coast defense artillery. MacArthur brought along his wife and young son, who would live in the tunnels of Corregidor along with the servicemen. MacArthur would spend almost the entire Bataan Campaign in the tunnels of Corregidor, managing the war from far in the rear echelon. Only once would he actually set foot on Bataan proper. Even then, he was far from the front lines. Despite this, MacArthur would send press releases back to the United States, in which his public affairs officers would lead President Roosevelt and the American public to believe he was on the front lines. In fact, less than half of MacArthur's messages to America would even mention his troops.

After abandoning Manila, MacArthur declared it an open city, and had the declaration announced through civilian radio stations. The "open city" declaration was an old concept in warfare. It meant that the defender was relinquishing the city without contest, and leaving it to the enemy. The open city declaration was designed to minimize civilian casualties by avoiding urban warfare. The Japanese did not recognize the concept, and bombed Manila anyway.

The retreat to Bataan would be in the worst of circumstances for an untrained army: a fighting retreat. As First Sergeant Jose and his machine gunners tried to hold off the Japanese advance, Third Lieutenant Arcadio and his cannons began to move south to Bataan. Arcadio's 155mm cannons were the most valuable artillery pieces on Luzon; they were also the slowest moving. As such, Arcadio's 301st Artillery was among the first units to displace to Bataan. Though the men rode in trucks, the cannons were towed by caterpillar tracked prime movers, which needed to stop periodically to keep from overheating.

As Jose fought, and Arcadio herded his cannons south, Primitivo, Domingo and Frederico were in reserve with the Philippine Scouts. With the defense of the beaches impossible, and the reinstatement of War Plan Orange, MacArthur ordered the Scouts back; their expertise would be needed later in the campaign.

When the combined Filipino-American forces reached the peninsula, the Battle for Bataan began in earnest. In many ways, there were actually two campaigns for Bataan, as a north-south mountain range separated MacArthur's forces. On the west side of Bataan, the Filipino-American forces were grouped in the I Corps, under the command of Major General Jonathan Wainwright. A career cavalryman and former commander of the Philippine Scouts, Wainwright's troops were almost all Philippine Commonwealth Troops, with a smattering of US Army Air Force troops who had been pressed into service as Infantry. Also serving under Wainwright was First Sergeant Jose and the 1st Regular Division. The 1st Regular Division occupied the I Corps main line of resistance, from the center of Bataan west to the coastal *barrio* of Mauban (Morton, 1953 & Whitman, 1990).

On the east side of Bataan, the II Corps was commanded by Brigadier General George Parker. Parker and his troops had just arrived on Bataan after desperately trying to stop the Japanese amphibious assaults in the south of Luzon. Among the troops assigned to Parker's corps was the Philippine Scouts and Arcadio's 301st Field Artillery.

Parker's main line of resistance stretched from the *barrio* of Abucay, on the banks of Manila Bay, west across a huge sugar plantation called Abucay Hacienda. Anchoring the right flank was the 57th Infantry (PS), including a Corporal Primitivo who had yet to see combat. The 57th's position lay astride the East Road, as General Parker believed that road was the probable attack route of the Japanese Army. Meanwhile, Private Domingo and Corporal Frederico, with the rest of the 45th Infantry (PS), remained in reserve.

General Parker's hunch was correct, as the Japanese Army sent their troops straight down the East Road. Incredibly, the Japanese troops were marching in columns, as if on parade, rather than spread out in combat formations. The Scouts manning the outpost positions called back to the artillery on field phones, and requested fire missions. Well back of the Abucay Hacienda, Third Lieutenant Arcadio and his 301st Field Artillery received the outpost's calls for fire, and responded quickly. Within minutes, huge 155mm high explosive shells rained down on the Japanese. The initial Japanese advance was obliterated, but the Japanese were only stopped temporarily. Subsequent advances brought the Japanese closer to the Scouts' lines; with the high rate of fire of their new M1 rifles, the Scouts decimated the Japanese infantry.

The oft-used Japanese tactic in the Philippines was to move forward until their troops ran into Filipino resistance. Then the Japanese would move laterally along the main line of resistance, looking for weak spots in the Filipino lines. They would infiltrate through the Filipino's weak points, and attack from the rear—a military tactic called the *envelopment*. After their initial destruction at the hands of the 301st Field Artillery and the 57th Infantry (PS) troops holding the East Road, the Japanese began probing for weakness

The Japanese slid west, away from the 57th, and towards the interior of Bataan. Along the way, they managed to pierce the Filipino lines on multiple occasions. At first, Commonwealth Army regiments held in reserve were fed into the line. But they lacked the training and motivation to solidify the front. Consequently, General Parker committed the 45th Infantry (PS) to shore up the front lines. Each time the Commonwealth lines broke, the Scouts would march into the fray, through the chaos of retreating Filipino forces, and stop the Japanese advance. But with each assault, the Scouts would lose more irreplaceable troops.

In an attempt to outflank the Filipino lines, the Japanese commander, Major General Homma Masaharu, sent his 9th Infantry Regiment to the far west end of the Filipino lines at Mount Natib. The 9th Infantry was supposed to assault the end of the Filipino lines, but became lost in the thick Bataan jungle. They wandered lost for days before finally breaking out of the thick jungle. The Japanese were surprised to find that they were behind the Abucay Line; behind the Filipinos. Hard fighting ensued, sometimes hand-to-hand. The Filipino troops carried a type of machete called a *bolo*. Intended as a farm implement for cutting rice, the Filipino troops found it to be an ideal night-fighting weapon, as they could noiselessly kill the Japanese soldiers.

Despite the bravery of the Filipino troops, the Japanese flanking movement bent back II Corps' lines. By January 17th, 1942, the Abucay Line had been bent back until it formed an inverted "L". General Parker, realizing he was in danger of having his corps cut off, called for a general retreat to the next line of defense. Though the Filipino-American forces would hold out for almost three more months, the campaign for the

Abucay Line was their high-water mark. After the Abucay battles, sickness and starvation would begin to take a heavier toll on the Filipinos than the Japanese would. Only on the Abucay Line would the Japanese battle a healthy Filipino army.

On the west side of Bataan, the situation was slightly better for the Filipino and U.S. forces of I Corps. Because the route was better on east Bataan, the majority of Japanese troops were committed there, against the Abucay Line. In the western I Corps, the Philippine Commonwealth Army was holding their positions. Rather than try a series of frontal assaults, the Japanese decided on more ingenious plans to bypass the Commonwealth lines.

Their first Japanese attempt resulted in the Battle of the Points, which took place over three weeks in January and February, 1942. Having learned at Abucay Hacienda that they could not steamroller through the Filipinos, the Japanese attempted to bypass the Filipinos via the sea. Using landing barges, the Japanese landed their 20th Infantry Regiment at three locations: Anyasan Point, Quinauan Point, and

Longaskawayan Point (Rottman, 2010). These three "points," which were rocky fingers of land jutting into the South China Sea, were guarded by Filipino police officers and US Army Air Force personnel who had no airplanes to service. When the Japanese 20th Infantry climbed the points, the ad hoc police and air force units held just long enough for General Wainwright to call for reinforcements.

MacArthur responded by sending parts of the 45th and 57th Infantry. The scouts of the 45th, with Private Domingo and Corporal Primitivo, boarded bright yellow *Pambusco* city buses for the trip to the west side of Bataan. Though most were suffering from malaria and dysentery, and *all* were slowly starving, their morale was high. After disembarking from the buses, they marched towards "the points" singing *Pinoy* rice harvesting songs. As they neared the points, the phrase *Petay si la*—"They shall die" was repeated amongst the Scouts. In rugged combat that was often hand-to-hand, the Scouts destroyed the Japanese 20th Infantry. The victory was pyrrhic, as the Scouts lost excellent troops who could not be replaced. Among the wounded was Private Primitivo, who would receive the first of three Purple Heart Medals for wounds sustained during the war.

While some of the Japanese troops landed at the points, others were trying to infiltrate directly through the Filipino lines. Their objective was to sneak through the Filipino lines, and occupy positions across the West Road, cutting off the Filipino's route of retreat. One Japanese infantry battalion managed to infiltrate through the remnants of the hard-fighting Filipino 1st Regular Division—First Sergeant Jose's division. The 1st Regular Division had been in combat for two solid months, and had lost most of their equipment. Jose related that they were surviving on handfuls of rice, with the occasional can of salmon.

As with the Battle of the Points, the Japanese troops who infiltrated the Filipino lines were unable to capitalize on their success. They were quickly surrounded in two "pockets of resistance," thus giving the battle its name (Morton, 1953). Philippine national police officers and the ad hoc unit of US Army Air Force personnel were joined by the 45th and 57th Infantry

Regiments (PS), who yet again was asked to destroy the Japanese.

I Corps' destruction of the Japanese during the Battles of the Pockets and Points, was a victory that prolonged, but did not win, the campaign. Though semi-independent, the actions of I Corps and II Corps were linked. If one Corps was forced back, the other would also have to pull back as well, to prevent being flanked and cut off. This was the theme of the Battle of Bataan: the Filipino-American forces slowly giving ground to Japanese penetrations. The Filipinos would then pull back and re-form their lines, and the cycle would begin again.

But with each passing day, the Bataan situation became more and more critical. On March 11th, 1942, MacArthur, his family, and eighteen members of his staff left the Philippines via Navy patrol boats. Also accompanying MacArthur was Philippine President Quezon, Vice President Osmena and Chief Justice Abad-Santo. The news was devastating to the Filipino and American defenders of Bataan. The American soldiers were amazed and depressed, as they could not conceive of a military leader leaving his army in the middle of a battle. The Filipinos, however, held out hope that MacArthur was leaving to find reinforcements. Command passed from General MacArthur to General Wainwright. As Wainwright assumed command on Corregidor, the Bataan command was passed to General King, Wainwright's chief of artillery.

In addition to the escape of the high command, the final defense of Bataan was hampered by the lack of supplies. As was typical in modern warfare, the rear echelon troops ate the best, and the frontline soldiers received the least rations. While Corregidor had crates of the standard army "c-rations," frontline soldiers were slowly starving. Infantrymen directly fighting the Japanese were subsisting on two handfuls of rice a day. They supplemented their diet by shooting monkeys out of trees, and hunting pythons and lizards. Others ate grass and insects.

While the lack of food was critical, the lack of medical supplies was equally devastating. Supplies of quinine and bandages were acute from the start of the campaign. Soldiers who were already weakened by hunger were destroyed by malaria and dysentery. Ultimately, the American commander on Bataan, General King, realized that prolonging the defense of Bataan would only lead to the death of more of his soldiers. They were too weak to effect change on the battlefield.

On April ninth, 1942, King surrendered Bataan, having been assured by General Homma Masaharu that the Filipino and U.S. soldiers would be treated humanely. Corregidor would hold out for one more month before those forces also surrendered.

Historians who have written about the Bataan Campaign unanimously subscribe to the thesis that it was lack of supplies, and not the Japanese military, that doomed the Filipino forces. Historians point to the lack of motorized transport for troop mobility; lack of medical evacuation of the wounded; and lack of modern firearms.

Interestingly, the Filipino veterans I interviewed are divided on whether or not they had proper supplies. Some do not believe lack of supplies was an issue;

they believed they had the proper equipment necessary. Others say the exact opposite: that they would never have stopped fighting had supplies held out.

None of the Filipino veterans I interviewed believed that the Japanese soldiers were superior to the Filipinos. This is interesting when compared to the American view of the Japanese soldier. In part, this seems to be a by-product of propaganda. The Filipinos first saw the Japanese (quite literally) down the sights of their rifles. The Filipinos did not have time to develop a fear of the Japanese soldier. By contrast, most Americans first became acquainted with the Japanese military in the days after Pearl Harbor. Propaganda was portraying the Japanese soldier with adjectives that were animalistic in nature; that they were cunning warriors temperamentally suited for fighting in the jungle. As most Americans who entered the military in the wake of Pearl Harbor did not go overseas for another two years, this gave the propaganda that much more time to sink in. These American soldiers who would meet the Japanese in combat in 1943 or 1944 would then learn what the

Filipinos had learned on Bataan: that the Japanese soldiers were beatable.

None of the Filipino veterans I interviewed blamed the senior US leadership for the defeat. General MacArthur, who fled the Philippines in March of 1942, is roundly criticized by American veterans of the Bataan Campaign. But I have not found any Filipino veterans—either through interviews or written sources—who dislike MacArthur. In large part this is because the Filipino veterans focus on MacArthur's positives: namely that he returned to the Philippines and liberated it. American veterans I have been fortunate to interview, by contrast, focus on the glaring fact that MacArthur left the battle in the middle of the campaign.

The Bataan Death March

The Filipino and American forces received word of their surrender in dribs and drabs, as the surrender message made its way from unit to unit. Some Filipino units were given time to destroy their weapons and gather food supplies, while other units were hastily told to march up the road to the nearest Japanese army unit and surrender.

First Sergeant Jose's unit was among those who had time to destroy their weapons. Jose and his men dug a long trench, disassembled their machine guns, and threw the pieces into the trench. Jose stood staring into the ditch, holding his .45 caliber pistol. A twice-wounded professional soldier who had fought the length of Luzon, Jose saw the surrender of his sidearm as quitting. He was about to hide his pistol in the waistband of his pants when his commanding officer pointed into the distance. On a small hill overlooking the Filipino positions, a group of Japanese officers were watching the *Pinoys* through binoculars. From the angle of the binocular lenses, Jose believed that they were looking directly at him.

A proud man, the First Sergeant began to disassemble his pistol while looking back at the Japanese. He threw the pieces of the pistol off into the jungle; if he could not have his pistol, he would make sure the Japanese did not get it, either. With that act of personal defiance done, Jose helped his men fill in the long trench, and then marched off with them to captivity.

For Third Lieutenant Arcadio, there were no weapons to destroy. The 301st Field Artillery had slowly lost all but one of their enemy cannons to enemy fire—mostly strikes by the Japanese Air Force. Instead, Lieutenant Arcadio merely gathered his men, and began walking towards the surrender point. By the point of surrender, Arcadio was so terribly wracked with malaria, dysentery and starvation that he was barely cognizant.

In many ways, First Sergeant Jose and Third Lieutenant Arcadio were lucky, as they were not immediately murdered by the Japanese soldiers. In one Philippine Commonwealth Army unit, the 91st Division, all the officers and senior sergeants were bound with telephone wire, and systematically slaughtered. At one end, Japanese enlisted soldiers stabbed the Filipinos with bayonets; at the other end of the line, Japanese officers beheaded the bound troops with samurai swords.

Among the Philippine Scouts, the surrender was particularly bitter. At every turn, they had valiantly fought the Japanese. Along the Abucay Line, at The Points and The Pockets, the 45th and 57th Infantry Regiments (PS) had been in every major engagement on Bataan. In head to head battles, in so many firefights they had lost track, the Scouts had always acquitted themselves with a professional soldiers honor. Now, they too disassembled their M1 rifles, and flung the parts off into the jungle. When they surrendered, the Japanese separated the Filipino sergeants and enlisted soldiers from the American officers, to keep them from communicating escape plans. It would be the last time the officers would see their soldiers until after the war; sometimes, forever.

Under Japanese guard, the Filipino prisoners were marched north, from the Bataan peninsula to the town of San Fernando. The distance of the trip varied for each group, depending on their start point. But an average distance of 60 miles was typical. Thus, the Bataan Death March was really a series of marches, as groups of prisoners were systematically moved to prisons. In a painful irony, many of the prisons the

Japanese chose to utilize were former Philippine Commonwealth Army bases. Pinoy soldiers found themselves returned to their former camps, in a much different state.

The march was intolerable for soldiers who had spent the previous weeks slowly starving to death. No rations or water was supplied by the Japanese; each Filipino had only the supplies they had when they surrendered. Often, the Japanese soldiers confiscated this food and water, as well as anything else the Japanese guard found desirable. Soldiers were killed for wedding rings, for toothbrushes and soap. One Japanese soldier confiscated an American officer's bottle of sleeping pills. Apparently thinking more is better, the Japanese soldier swallowed the entire contents of the bottle—and quickly died.

In many prisoner groups, soldiers were not allowed to help each other. Each Filipino prisoner had to move under his own motive power. Any soldier who could not walk on his own, or who fell behind the group, was executed and left in the road. Thus, subsequent prisoner groups would march north past the bodies of their fellow soldiers. Japanese motor transport and tanks, moving south, would drive over the bodies in the roads.

Third Lieutenant Arcadio was one of these soldiers who could not walk on his own. A popular officer who had a deep sense of duty to this troops, there was no shortage of Filipino enlisted soldiers to prop him up. Luckily, he was in a prisoner group that allowed soldiers to help each other. He would later relate to me that he had no real memory of walking the Bataan Death March, because he was delirious the whole time.

In another prisoner group, First Sergeant Jose and the machine gunners of Company M, 1st Regular Division was also walking north. Filipino women would line roads, or come out of their houses, to bring food and water to the prisoners. The Japanese guards would chase the women away; in some case, they would execute the women trying to help the Filipino prisoners-of-war. Without their help, many of the Filipino prisoners would die; with their help, many would live. First Sergeant Jose would see soldiers fall dead while marching: "Some of them just fell down in the road, from tiredness and nothing to eat."

The Bataan Death March began with roughly 17,000 American soldiers and 70,000 *Pinoys*. During the march, it is estimated that 600 Americans and 5-to-10,000 Filipinos died (Knox, 1981). Casualties are at best a guess, since the Japanese did not maintain any records. Further, Philippine Commonwealth soldiers were not issued with any type of identity tags, such as the US Army "dog tags." Because of this, it was nearly impossible to identify the bodies of Filipino soldiers, leading to shockingly high amounts of "unknown soldiers."

Eventually, Jose's group reached the final leg of the Bataan Death March: the *barrio* of San Fernando. Located just north of the point where the Bataan peninsula connects to the rest of Luzon, San Fernando was a major rail hub. If the prisoners thought their ordeal was about to end, they were sadly mistaken. At San Fernando they were packed into box cars that were padlocked from the outside. The trains then headed further north, into Luzon's interior. Their final destination was Camp O'Donnell, a former Philippine Commonwealth Army base. Not knowing what to do with the prisoners of war, the Japanese incarcerated them in O'Donnell for the next half year, while the prisoners died of starvation and disease.

Third Lieutenant Arcadio survived the Bataan Death March through the good graces of his soldiers, who propped him up between them, to keep him marching. He would also survive imprisonment in Camp O'Donnell. However, his health would be ruined by the malaria and dysentery. After his release from prison in mid-1942, he would return home to recuperate.

First Sergeant Jose, by contrast, never made it to prison. He reached San Fernando, and watched as other prisoners were jammed into train cars. Standing with Jose were the last fifteen members of Company M. During the initial defense near Lingayan Gulf, down the length of Luzon, and the bloody battles for the Pockets, Company M had lost about 135 soldiers. The last surviving members of Company M asked their senior Sergeant what they should do. Jose, who never wanted to quit fighting, told his troops he was most definitely not getting into the box cars. When the Japanese guards were not looking, Jose and his men darted off into the jungle. While in the jungle, the remants of M Company split up, as all wanted to go home and check on their families. First Sergeant Jose also left to check on his family—then headed into the jungles of Luzon to join the guerrillas. By contrast, Corporal Primitivo spent seven months slowly starving in prison at Camp O'Donnell. Eventually the Japanese released him, but there was no way for him to return to his family on the island of Panay. Instead he headed to Batangas Province, where he helped form a guerrilla unit that specialized in communications.

Organizational Structure of Pinoy Guerrilla Units

Twentieth century guerrilla warfare tends to revolve around the three-step Maoist guerrilla model, in which the insurgents begin as guerrillas as they slowly build up a parallel government to that which is in power. As that level is achieved, the guerrilla army transforms into a conventional army, which is capable of installing the parallel government. In the instance of the Philippines, however, Maoist doctrine never took hold, though the guerrilla works of Mao Tse Tung were available to the Filipino-American guerrilla bands (Ramsey, 2005). Rather, the Filipinos were in a position in which they could fight a pure guerrilla war. For the *Pinoys*, it was "pure" in the sense that they did not need to build a conventional army, or attempt to overthrow the government. They needed only to fight.

Instead, the *Pinoys* were fortunate (relatively speaking) in that they only had to fulfill the primary tenet of guerrilla warfare: to just keep living. They had to last until General MacArthur fulfilled his pledge to return and liberate the Philippines. For the Filipino guerrillas, every day that they continued to exist was a victory. As long as the Filipino people knew that somewhere, out in the jungle, armed men were refusing to bow to the Japanese, then they could continue to withstand the humiliations heaped on them by the occupation.

Years after the war, when General MacArthur was writing his memoirs, he would claim that it was his idea to form a guerrilla army to continue the fight against the Japanese. He would write in his autobiography *Reminiscences,* that he came up with the idea for a guerrilla army during the Bataan Campaign, when he was still in command of the Filipino-American forces. This appears to be a revision on MacArthur's part, as there are no official Army orders of equipment requisitions or troop movements that point to the establishment of an official guerrilla operation. In fact, three of the most effective guerrilla leaders: Lieutenant Robert Lapham, Lieutenant Edwin Ramsey, and Sergeant Ray Hunt, wrote in *their* autobiographies that they became guerrilla leaders almost by accident.

While none of the guerrilla bands appear to have been pre-planned, they all had the same sort of schematic—a sort of organizational DNA that allowed them to flourish.

First, the bands had a multitude of members who had been in the military during the Bataan Campaign. On the surface, this would seem obvious, given the breadth and depth of Filipino mobilization during the early days of the Japanese invasion. But on another level, the presence of veterans was fortunate.[4] The guerrilla bands were able to start off with combat experienced members, and the learning curve of combat was almost non-existent.

Frederico, the Philippine Scout Corporal who had fought at Abucay Hacienda, joined the guerrillas in northern Luzon as soon as he was paroled from Camp O'Donnell. Frederico related that to me that he and his fellow guerrillas never really needed to learn to be guerrillas; they merely continued fighting as Philippine Scouts, utilizing the same Infantry tactics they had used during the Bataan Campaign.

Second, all of the successful guerrilla bands—and in this case "success" means they were still around when the United States Army returned—had the support of the civilian population. Since most of the guerrillas tended to operate from their home areas, civilian support often came about because of kinship ties.[5] In

---

[4] As comparison, the Polish underground army, Armia Krajowa, also found that the large presence of military veterans was a key to operational effectiveness. In contrast, the Viet Minh in Southeast Asia had a steeper learning curve, as they were prohibited from joining the French military.

[5] On the other hand, the most brutal punishment the guerrillas meted out was often to family members who

other cases, civilian support was received *after* the guerrillas were able to demonstrate their guerrilla operations would benefit the populace.

With the breakdown of civil government, criminal bands were rampant in the Philippine countryside. In many cases, the first act of the guerrilla bands was to eliminate the criminals. Sometimes this was done by incorporating the marauders into the guerrilla band—essentially harnessing the energy of the criminals for a greater good. In other cases, the guerrillas merely beheaded the criminals, and the case was closed.

Third, the guerrilla bands were tied—often tenuously—to the US Army. After MacArthur set up his headquarters in Australia, he assigned a full-time liaison officer to the guerrillas. The liaison unit would come to be known as the Allied Intelligence Bureau (AIB). The AIB was tasked with ensuring that the guerrillas were supplied with necessary equipment. But more importantly, the AIB was responsible for intelligence coming out of the Philippines. This is what betrayed the guerrilla cause.

MacArthur really wanted: quality intelligence on Japanese troop dispositions, for use when the American forces returned to retake the Philippines.

For a guerrilla band to succeed, it helped to be acknowledged by the US Army, via the AIB. Recognition came about once the AIB determined that the guerrilla band was "reliable" (i.e., pro-American). For the most part, recognition was relatively easy, as most of the guerrilla bands were either led by a white American officer, or had a predominance of former Philippine Commonwealth or Philippine Scout members. Once they were "anointed," the guerrilla bands could receive supplies and arms from the US Army--a safer alternative than taking weapons from the Japanese (Breuer, 2005).

Fourth, the primary purpose of the guerrilla bands was intelligence gathering. As already mentioned, MacArthur saw the worth of the guerrillas as purveyors of intelligence—what would become known as the "bamboo telegraph." To aid in the intelligence gathering, Filipino-Americans who had joined the US Army in the days after Pearl Harbor were recruited as radio operators. They were infiltrated into the Philippines, where they were stationed with the guerrilla bands. There the radio operators would send daily updates on the comings and goings of the Japanese Army.

However, this is not to imply that the guerrilla bands were avoiding directly fighting the Japanese. In multiple occasions, *Pinoy* guerrillas would directly confront the Japanese, often with devastating results. Private Primitivo, who fought the Japanese in Batangas Province, noted matter-of-factly that the guerrillas would behead the dead Japanese soldiers, as a sign of their hatred for the Japanese.

Another example of direct action against the Japanese was related by by Corporal Frederico, who fought in a guerrilla band in north Luzon; as was typical with the guerrillas I interviewed, he picked the guerrilla band closest to his home and family. By the beginning of 1944, Corporal Frederico had been at war for three years; two as a guerrilla. In February, 1944, Frederico would lead his guerrilla band out of the Cordillera Mountains, to raid a Japanese garrison on the Luzon plains. The Japanese had intensified their patrol operations, and Frederico had devised a plan to check their movements. His plan was a direct action raid on the Japanese base, a move designed to destroy the Japanese sense of safety while sapping their motivation to leave their fortress. After all, if they could were not safe in their own barracks, they were not safe *anywhere* in the Philippines. Frederico's raid was a success, and the guerrillas ceased to have difficulties with the Japanese army. Frederico, who retired from the U.S. Army decades later as a Major, received the Bronze Star for Valor for his leadership during the raid. But the true worth of the operation was the fact that Frederico's guerrilla band could now move about the countryside with impunity. In that small corner of the Luzon plains, the Japanese Army was occupiers in name only.

Likewise, Jose and his guerrilla band would also actively fight the Japanese. Jose was a member of the guerrilla band located in Nueva Ecija province. The commander of the guerrilla army, American Robert Lapham, had been a Lieutenant in the Philippine Scouts. Lapham's guerrillas would assist the US

Army's 6th Ranger Battalion on a daring raid on the Cabanatuan POW camp. The raid, which took place in the spring of 1945, after the American army returned to the Philippines, would free over 500 American prisoners.

Jose had been specially brought on the mission because he had been born and raised in the area around Cabanatuan. Jose's guerrilla detachment was tasked with holding off Japanese reinforcements, while the Rangers evacuated the POW's. Jose would later describe the battle between guerrillas and the Japanese:

"We are protecting the road, in case the Japanese attack. If the Japanese know about it [the raid on Cabanatuan] and they raid it, they can easily go in there and the whole raid will fail. They [the Rangers and POWs] would all be slaughtered in there."

The slaughter never happened, as the guerrilla ambush completely stopped the Japanese reinforcements from reaching the Cabanatuan POW camp. Jose, the former First Sergeant turned guerrilla leader, had helped save 500 near-death American prisoners. In doing so, he had lifted the burden of *walang hiya.*

Five months after the joint Ranger-guerrilla raid on Cabanatuan, World War Two ended in the Pacific. Jose, Frederico, Primitivo and Domingo who had been in combat since the beginning of the war, laid down their arms, and came out of the jungle. However, their service was not over: the *Pinoys* would need them to help build a free, independent Philippine Republic.

Chapter Six: A Checkpoint in San Manuel

This project is the culmination of six years of research into the Filipino guerrilla experience. It began when my father told me the story of his grandfather, who was stabbed to death by a Japanese soldier in 1942. It happened at a checkpoint near San Manuel, Luzon, Philippines. No one in my family is really sure why *LoLo* was killed, just that his life was taken by a bayonet thrust to the back. My Grandfather Antonio and his brother Rudolfo, both living in America, tried their hardest to join the US Navy to fight their way back to the Philippines. But at the time, the Navy was not interested in minorities, only white sailors.

These family stories were my impetus for learning about the Filipino guerrilla experience—the men and women who refused to die at Japanese checkpoints. The more I delved into the history of the World War Two Philippines, the more I interviewed the *Pinoy* veterans, the more I came to realize that these were special people. They would shake their heads and object if I called them *bayani* (hero), but these veterans *were* reluctant heroes, whose road to liberation was strewn with loss and heartache, but finally victory.

Whether or not one is Filipino, we all owe the *Pinoy guerrilerros* our gratitude. In their quest for an independent Philippines; in their motivation to stand against invasion, they helped defeat fascism and ensure a free world.

References

Aguinaldo, E (2010). *True Version of the Philippine*

    Revolution. Laverne: General Books.

Breuer, W. (2005). *MacArthur's Secret War.* Edison:

    Castle Books.

Breuer, W. (2002). *The Great Raid.* New York:

    Miramax Books.

Bulosan, Carlos (1995). *The Cry and the Dedication.*

    Philadelphia: Temple University Press.

Costello, J. (1981). *The Pacific War: 1941-1945.*

    New York: Harper Collins.

Department of the Army (1966). *Human Factors*

    Considerations of Undergrounds in Insurgencies.
    Government Published.

Department of the Army (2006). *Counterinsurgency.*

    Government Published.

Department of the Army (1966). *Selected Readings in*

Guerrilla and Counterguerrilla Operations.

Government published.

Department of the Army (2009). *Guerrilla Warfare.*

Government Published.

Department of the Army (1986). *Counterguerrilla*

Operations. Government Published.

Duncan, H. (2006). *Holocaust in Manila.* USA: Trafford

Publishing.

Gurr, T. (1970). *Why Men Rebel.* Princeton: Princeton

University Press.

Hoyt, E. (2001). *Japan's War*. New York: Cooper

Square Publishing.

Hunt, R. and Norling, B. (1986). *Behind Japanese*

Lines. New York: Pocket Books.

Jessup, J. and Coakley, R. (1979). *A Guide to the Study and Use of Military History.* Published by the US Army.

Jose, R. (1992). *The Philippine Army, 1935-1942.* Manila: Ateneo de Manila University Press.

Kessler, R. (1989). *Rebellion and Repression in the Philippines.* New Haven: Yale University Press.

Knox, D. (1981). *Death March.* New York: Harcourt Books.

Lapham, R. and Norling, B. (1996). *Lapham's Raiders.* Lexington: University Of Kentucky Press.

de Lara, R. (2000). *Boy Guerrilla.* Lincoln: iUniverse.

Laqueur, W. (1976). *Guerrilla*. Boston: Little, Brown and Company.

Liddell-Hart, B. (1991) *Strategy.* New York: Henry Holt & Company.

MacArthur, D. (1964). *Reminiscences.* Greenwich:

Fawcett Publishers.

Mallonee, R. (1997). *Battle for Bataan.* Novato:

Presidio Press.

McKinley, W. (2006). *Compilation of the Messages and*

Papers of the Presidents: William McKinley.

Charleston: Bibliobazaar.

Miller, S. (1982). *Benevolent Assimilation.* New Haven:

Yale University.

Morrett, J. (1993). *Soldier Priest.* Roswell: Old Rugged

Cross Press.

Morton, L. (1953). *The Fall of the Philippines.*

Washington, D.C.: Published by the US Army.

Norman, E. (1999). *We Band of Angels.* New York:

Simon & Schuster.

Oberschall, A. (1997). *Social Movements.* New

    Brunswick: Transaction Publishers.

Olson, J. (1991). *Anywhere-Anytime: The History of*

    the 57th Infantry (PS). Self-published.

O'Neill, B. (1990). *Insurgency & Terrorism.*

    Washington: Brassy's (US), Inc.

Pabico, R. (2006). *The Exiled Government.* New York:

    Humanity Books.

Parsa, Misagh (2000). *States, Ideologies, & Social*

    Revolutions. Cambridge: Cambridge University

    Press.

de Quesada, A. (2007). *The Spanish-American War*

    and Philippine Insurrection. Oxford: Osprey
    Publishing.

Ramsey, E. and Rivele, S. (2005). *Lieutenant Ramsey's*

    War. Washington, D.C.: Potomac Books, Inc.

Record, J. (2009). *Beating Goliath: Why Insurgencies Fail.* Dulles: Potomac Books.

Recto, C. (1946). *Three Years of Enemy Occupation.* Manila: People's Press.

Rice, E. (1988). *Wars of the Third Kind: Conflict in Underdeveloped Countries.* Berkeley: University of California Press.

Rio, E. (1999). *Rays of a Setting Sun*. Manila: LaSalle Press.

Rottman, G. (2009) *World War II US Cavalry Units: Pacific Theatre.* Oxford: Osprey Publishing.

San Juan, E. (1986). *Crisis in the Philippines.* South Hadley: Bergin and Garvey Books.

Sides, H. (2001). *Ghost Soldiers.* New York: Anchor Books.

Skocpol, T. (1979). *States and Social Revolutions*.

Cambridge: Cambridge University Press.

Stahl, B. (1995). *You're No Good to Me Dead.*

Annapolis: Naval Academy Press.

Stanton, S. (2006). *The US Army Order of Battle.*

Mechanicsburg: Stackpole Books.

Steinberg, D. (1967) Philippine Collaboration in WWII.

Ann Arbor: University of Michigan Press.

Taggaro, S. (1991). *All This Was Bataan.* Quezon City:

New Day Publishers.

Tenney, L. (2007). *My Hitch in Hell: The Bataan Death*

March. Washington, D.C.: Potomac Books.

Terkel, S. (1984). *The Good War.* New York: The New

Press.

Tilly, L. and Tilly, C. (1975). *The Rebellious Century.*

Cambridge: Harvard University Press.

Tse-Tung, M. (2005). *On Guerrilla Warfare* (S. Griffith,

Trans.) Minneola: Dover Publications.

US Army (1931). War *Department Circular No. 41*.

Government published.

US Army (1941). *War Department Bulletin No. 20*.

Government published.

US Army (1941). *The Soldier's Handbook*.

Government published.

US Army (1944). *Tagalog*. Government Published.

Whitehead, K. (2006) *Odyssey of a Philippine Scout.*

Bedford: Aberjona Press.

Whitman, J. (1990). *Bataan: Our Last Ditch.* New

York: Hippocrene Books.

Wolfert, I. (1980). *American Guerrilla In The

Philippines.* New York: Bantam Books.

Young, D. (2009). *The Battle of Bataan.* Jefferson:

MacFarland and Company.

Appendix A: Veteran's Questionnaire

Dear Veteran:

Thank you for taking part in my survey! I consider it a profound honor that you are willing to share your life story with me, and I am grateful.

I am a second generation Filipino-American, currently a graduate student in Political and Justice Studies, at Governors State University. My thesis is about the soldiers who served in the Philippine Army, Philippine Scouts, and Philippine Constabulary during World War Two.

My primary goal is to collect and preserve the personal stories of veterans such as you, as your valor and devotion to duty was a prime reason the Japanese were defeated. I hope that by recording these stories, I can contribute to the historical legacy of Filipino veterans.

My secondary goal is to make the veterans' stories accessible to the American public. I want Americans to understand that in the Philippines, World War Two didn't stop with Bataan and pick up again with the American invasion at Lingayan gulf. Rather, the Filipino people were continuously in the war from 1941 to 1945.

In the enclosed survey, I have asked a number of general questions—about you, your background, and your military service. By using a survey format, I can ask each veteran the same standardized questions, and get a range of answers.

As a combat veteran of the Iraq War, I understand that speaking about wartime experiences can be difficult. With that in mind, I have tried to develop non-intrusive questions. That being said, please feel free to skip any questions that you do not want to answer.

If you have any questions or comments about the questionnaire or my thesis, please feel free to contact me. Please let me repeat that I am both humbled and grateful for your military service, and for your assistance in this project.

Respectfully,

Matthew Cenon Andres

818 Dighton Lane

Schaumburg, IL 60173

This section asks for generalized information.

Name:

_____

_____

_____

Year of Birth:

_____

_____

_____

Home (Town / Province / Island):

_____

_____

_____

Occupation prior to enlistment:

_____

_____

_____

Years of Military Service:

_____

_____

_____

Rank:

_____

_____

_____

Military Unit (Regiment / Division):

_____

_____

_____

Geographic Areas of Service:

_____

_____

_____

Awards Received:

_____

_____

_____

The first section explores your general outlook during the war. The scale runs from 1 to 5. The number 1 represents complete disagreement with the statement. The number 5 represents complete agreement with the statement. The numbers 2, 3, and 4 represent various degrees of agreement or disagreement. Please circle whichever number best corresponds to your feelings.

1) I believe that President Quezon provided quality leadership during World War II.

    1 – I completely disagree with the statement

    2 – I somewhat disagree with the statement

    3 – I neither agree nor disagree with the statement

    4 – I somewhat agree with the statement

    5 – I completely agree with the statement

2) I believe that General MacArthur provided quality leadership during World War II.

    1 – I completely disagree with the statement

    2 – I somewhat disagree with the statement

    3 – I neither agree nor disagree with the statement

    4 – I somewhat agree with the statement

    5 – I completely agree with the statement

3) I believe that the **Filipino** officers I served directly under provided quality leadership.

    1 – I completely disagree with the statement

    2 – I somewhat disagree with the statement

    3 – I neither agree nor disagree with the statement

    4 – I somewhat agree with the statement

    5 – I completely agree with the statement

4) I believe that the **American** officers I served directly under provided quality leadership.

    1 – I completely disagree with the statement

    2 – I somewhat disagree with the statement

    3 – I neither agree nor disagree with the statement

    4 – I somewhat agree with the statement

    5 – I completely agree with the statement

5) I believe that the Filipino and American forces were properly equipped to repel the Japanese invasion.

    1 – I completely disagree with the statement

    2 – I somewhat disagree with the statement

    3 – I neither agree nor disagree with the statement

    4 – I somewhat agree with the statement

    5 – I completely agree with the statement

6) During the initial Japanese invasion of Luzon (1941-1942), I believe that the General Staff had a viable plan to defend the Philippines.

    1 – I completely disagree with the statement

    2 – I somewhat disagree with the statement

    3 – I neither agree nor disagree with the statement

    4 – I somewhat agree with the statement

    5 – I completely agree with the statement

7) Bataan would not have fallen, had adequate supplies been available.

    1 – I completely disagree with the statement

    2 – I somewhat disagree with the statement

    3 – I neither agree nor disagree with the statement

    4 – I somewhat agree with the statement

    5 – I completely agree with the statement

8) I agreed with General King's decision to surrender the Bataan based Filipino-American forces in 1942.

    1 – I completely disagree with the statement

    2 – I somewhat disagree with the statement

    3 – I neither agree nor disagree with the statement

    4 – I somewhat agree with the statement

    5 – I completely agree with the statement

Section 2

This section explores your attitude towards the Japanese military. It uses the same 1-to-5 scale as the earlier section. Please circle the number that corresponds to your answer.

8) I saw a distinction between the typical Japanese Army soldier and the Japanese Imperial High Command.

    1 – I completely disagree with the statement

    2 – I somewhat disagree with the statement

    3 – I neither agree nor disagree with the statement

    4 – I somewhat agree with the statement

    5 – I completely agree with the statement

9) I hated the Japanese for invading the Philippines.

    1 – I completely disagree with the statement

    2 – I somewhat disagree with the statement

    3 – I neither agree nor disagree with the statement

    4 – I somewhat agree with the statement

    5 – I completely agree with the statement

10) I still cannot forgive the Japanese for invading the Philippines.

    1 – I completely disagree with the statement

    2 – I somewhat disagree with the statement

    3 – I neither agree nor disagree with the statement

    4 – I somewhat agree with the statement

    5 – I completely agree with the statement

11) The Japanese Army was better equipped than the joint Filipino-American Army.

    1 – I completely disagree with the statement

    2 – I somewhat disagree with the statement

    3 – I neither agree nor disagree with the statement

    4 – I somewhat agree with the statement

    5 – I completely agree with the statement

12) The Japanese army was tactically superior to the joint Filipino-American army.

    1 – I completely disagree with the statement

    2 – I somewhat disagree with the statement

    3 – I neither agree nor disagree with the statement

    4 – I somewhat agree with the statement

    5 – I completely agree with the statement

13) The average Japanese soldier was tougher than the average Filipino soldier.

    1 – I completely disagree with the statement

    2 – I somewhat disagree with the statement

    3 – I neither agree nor disagree with the statement

    4 – I somewhat agree with the statement

    5 – I completely agree with the statement

Section 3

This last section contains cultural questions that cannot be answered on a fixed scale. Please answer in the space provided; feel free to add paper if you need more space for your answer.

The Philippines has a long and valiant history of resisting oppression by outside forces. Among the pantheon of Filipino heroes are Emilio Aguinaldo and Jose Rizal. Do you feel that this revolutionary past influenced you during World War Two? If so, was it a positive influence or a negative influence?

_____

_____

_____

_____

_____

_____

_____

_____

_____

_____

The Philippines was close to gaining its independence from the United States, but that independence was almost derailed by the Japanese invasion. At that time (1941-1945), the Japanese occupation seemed to slam the door on Philippine independence. Did the Filipino yearning for an independent country play a role in your thoughts and actions during World War Two?

_____

_____

_____

_____

_____

_____

_____

_____

_____

Patriotism is often defined as a love of country. When you think of your own patriotic feelings during World War Two, what seems most vivid?

_____

_____

_____

_____

_____

_____

_____

After the Filipino and American forces surrendered, did you take part in the Filipino guerrilla movement? If so, what was your motivation for continuing to fight the Japanese at a time when all hope seemed lost?

_____

_____

_____

_____

_____

_____

_____

_____

_____

What is your attitude towards your status as a veteran? Do you take part in parades or remembrances in which you wear identifying clothing or military medals? Are you a member of a veterans' organization?

_____

_____

_____

_____

_____

_____

_____

_____

Thank you for taking part in my survey. I deeply appreciate you taking the time and effort to share your life stories with me. As a Filipino-American, I have always been interested in the history of the Philippines. This thesis I am preparing is the pinnacle of that interest, and I am deeply honored by your assistance.

Salamat Po!

Matthew Cenon Andres

818 Dighton LN

Schaumburg, IL 60173

Tx.: (847)882-6594

About the author

Matthew Andres is an independent historian, who lives in northern Illinois. Matthew is a former police officer, and combat veteran of Operation Iraqi Freedom. Matthew owns Andres Historical Solutions, LLC, a public history firm specializing in 20th century U.S. political and military history. He can be reached via email at:

Information@andreshistorical.com

Made in the
USA
Middletown, DE